Camden History

Contents

The **Camden History Review** is published annually by the Camden History Society

c/o Camden Local Studies Centre
Holborn Library
32–28 Theobalds Road
London WC1X 8PA

Information about membership is available from this address.

© Copyright
Camden History Society and contributors 2001

ISBN 0-904491-51-X
ISSN 0305-4756 47-4

Edited by F Peter Woodford

Associate Editor David Hayes

Designed by Ivor Kamlish

Gene Adams	Mabel Quiller-Couch in Downshire Hill	2
David Hayes	"Without parallel in the known world": the chequered past of 277 Gray's Inn Road	5
A D Harvey	Bollards in Camden	10
Brian Cox, Bob Gilham & Peter G Scott	From stones to ohms: the history of electricity in Hampstead and the Central Supply Station, Lithos Road	12
David L Jones	The school for sons and orphans of missionaries in Mornington Crescent, 1852–7	16
William Barnes	A short history of Oak Village	18
Michael Alpert	The Irish in Kilburn, and the Church of the Sacred Heart, Quex Road	24
F Peter Woodford	Provident and non-provident dispensaries in Camden	28
Bryan Diamond	Architectural details on Hampstead houses	32
David Hellings	History of a late-20th-century development:: Kingswell, Hampstead, 1960–1995	37
Geraldine Charles	Keeley House (Keeley Street) and its predecessors	42
Robert Leon	Rise and fall of the Aerated Bread Company	47
	Corrigenda to CHR 24 , pp 6–11	11

The invariably helpful co-operation and assistance of the staff of the Camden Local Studies and Archive Centre is gratefully acknowledged.

Cover:
Lithos Road Annual outing, 1906. (see p 14)

Mabel Quiller-Couch in Downshire Hill

by Gene Adams

Most of us have some memory of the work of Sir Arthur Quiller-Couch, the distinguished Edwardian author and Cambridge professor who wrote under the name "Q", but very few will have heard of Mabel Quiller-Couch, one of his two sisters. Mabel, Lilian and Arthur had a long-standing and happy association with Hampstead in the first 30 years of the 20th century. The two sisters were residents of Downshire Hill; Q was a frequent visitor and, later, active in the campaign to save nearby Keats House. All three were writers: Mabel and Arthur wrote fiction with a distinctive, original quality; Mabel and Lilian wrote mainly for children. Lilian was married to J H Lobban, a lecturer in the English Department at Birkbeck College.

In 1905 Miss Mabel Quiller-Couch is listed as resident at 16 Downshire Hill. She lived there independently for 12 years, supporting herself as a children's author but helped financially by Q, who in a letter to her in 1921 hoped soon to be "a decent brother again" - apparently after a break in his contributions. Lilian and John Lobban moved into No.37, opposite No.16, in 1911.

Downshire Hill achieved completion in the early 19th century, and through vigilant local conservationists has maintained its Regency charm. Many of the houses at the upper end are straight out of Prinny's Brighton, with Gothick pinnacles and delicate iron balconies; nearer the Heath there are more modest semi-detached or terraced houses. Nos.16 and 17 form a pair of square brick semi-detached houses, marked in the centre of the façade with a painted stone bearing the legend *Portland Place 1823*, the only other decoration being an elegant fan window over each front door. Almost directly opposite is St John's Downshire Hill, a proprietary chapel built in the same year, 1823.

Downshire Hill still has the air of being on the edge of the countryside because of its proximity to the East Heath, and in Mabel's day this illusion must have been even more marked. Hampstead maintained its air of detachment from London until well into the 20th century, largely through the steepness of its hill which deterred cumbersome omnibuses, and in spite of the presence of Hampstead Heath station on the Hampstead Junction Railway (now North London Line) at South End Green connecting local residents to the City. Hampstead's growth spurt came with the arrival of the Underground in 1907, and Mabel must have seen many changes during her sojourn in Downshire Hill.

Childhood and early life

The Quiller-Couches spent their childhood in Cornwall and Devon, where their father Dr Thomas Quiller-Couch was a general practitioner in Bodmin. In Q's fragment of autobiography published posthumously in 1944 is a glimpse of the children's life in Bodmin, when they were taken to see a pantomime in the 'travelling Theatre Royal' – a kind of circus tent. As the local doctor's children they had reserved seats "distinguished by a covering of carpet". Afterwards, Q records they severely criticised the performance, for "apart from a nursery shelf of fairy tales, we had the run of our father's library, rich beyond common in poetry, romantic tales and folklore. I remember my elder sister [i.e. the elder of his two sisters, Mabel - she was actually younger than Q] being led away protesting after a performance of *The Babes in the Wood*. She had read the story in *The Ingoldsby Legends* and wanted ocular satisfaction of the Wicked Uncle's punishment that all he swallowed turned acid."

At Christmas they would be taken to the Theatre Royal at Plymouth. This was a much grander outing. Q "would be dragged into a haberdasher's to be fitted with white-kid gloves to suit my black evening velveteens, while [Mabel] had her lanky red hair 'frizzed' for the occasion". This cavalier brotherly description of Mabel's hair reveals that they all three had reddish hair, while their mother's was "deep auburn". The name Couch, of Cornish origin and pronounced *Cooch*, actually means red (see A L Rowse's biography of Q, p 10). In 1907 Mabel wrote a book, clearly based on the Quiller-Couch family's childhood, called *A Pair of Red Polls* (red heads). In his autobiography Q wrote "My grandfather...affected a sternness terrifying enough when he lectured us after one of our many childish scrapes, *vide* my sister Mabel's story *A Pair of Red Polls*". Which between you and me is one of my best [favourite] books...".

As well as sharing reddish hair, freckles and a tendency to read books, the children were touchingly shy and modest, characteristics that seemed to stay with them right to the end and probably had much to do with the general affection in which they were held. This shyness inhibited both Q and Mabel from writing directly about themselves, even in old age. Q's unfinished autobiography was wrung out of him by pleas from friends. But as Rowse pointed out, Q often used fiction to disguise writing that is in fact autobiographical (for example in *The Ship of Stars*, 1899). Mabel too used memories of her own childhood in her children's books. Her fiction was superior to her brother's in some respects, particularly in depth of psychological perception, but they were clearly both exceptionally sensitive and intelligent. Their sense of propriety and loyalty to their concept of family honour is difficult to describe today, when 'standards' are called snobbery or élitism, and the concept of duty has all but vanished.

Oxford days

In 1886 their father died and the family moved to Oxford in much reduced circumstances. The 13 years until Mrs Quiller-Couch (née Mary Ford) died were highly stressful for Mabel: as eldest daughter she had to cope with the spendthrift ways of their otherwise charming mother, who felt the degradation of becoming an Oxford landlady keenly. Then, according to Rowse, one of the younger brothers "went to the bad" in an undisclosed way. Rowse writes that from then on the two boys were "never mentioned in a family so bent on keeping up appearances or (to put it more kindly) standards.". In many ways, the death of her mother in 1899, when Mabel was about 35, must have come as a relief.

Mabel had already started writing for children. Her first book, *Martha's Trials: the Truth will Prevail*, was published by the Sunday School Union in 1895. In addition to the disgrace brought upon them by the younger brothers, it is said – though not substantiated – that at this time she suffered a disappointment in love from which she never fully recovered. Her niece Foy writing in 1979 added that she thought her aunt had taken to her bed in true Victorian fashion and remained an invalid for the rest of her life. However, our photographic evidence (see later) contradicts that, although it does indicate a declining state of health in the years before her death in 1924 (Fig 1).

Q left Oxford in 1887 to work for Cassell's, and lived in lodgings in Kensington. In 1889 he was married in Fowey where his first child, Bevil, was born in 1890. Q became a long-distance commuter, working frantically in London to support not only his new wife and child in Fowey but also his mother

1 Mabel Quiller-Couch and sister Lilian Lobban (in hat) with parlourmaid Mildred and cook Myrtle on Mabel's 56th birthday, 1920, in the garden of 37 Downshire Hill.

and two brothers at Oxford High School, not to mention paying off a huge debt run up by his deceased father. No wonder he soon suffered a serious breakdown; from 1891 onwards he gave up London and worked from Fowey, where he lived the rest of his life in a house called The Haven. When appointed professor of English at Cambridge in 1912 he resumed a split existence, living in Jesus College during term and Cornwall during vacations.

What drew Mabel to London, and to Hampstead?

It is possible that during his hectic life in London, Q made friends or acquaintances who lived in Hampstead. However that may be, when Mabel decided that London was a better base from which to contact publishing houses she would certainly have been drawn to the semi-rural nature of the town on the hill. Her little house at 16 Downshire Hill evidently became a 'haven' for her as well. From 1905 to 1917, when her poor health finally necessitated a move to her sister's at No.37, she worked away steadily, publishing 18 books for children. In one good year – 1910 – she actually published seven. Her total output from 1895 until her death was 55 published books, doubtless many articles in magazines or religious newsletters, and the normal output of any person properly brought up in Victorian times: carefully composed letters to friends or relations. Unlike Q, she did not attempt poetry.

Mabel's best writing is found in a number of the novels for young readers then known as *Girls' Stories*. But there was also a splendid anthology, edited jointly with Lilian, the 1911 *Book of Children's Verse*, well illustrated with full-page watercolours. The Preface is signed M.Q.-C. and L.Q.-C., Hampstead 1911, which establishes its Hampstead origin. The sisters thank several contemporary poets for allowing their work to be used, including two from Hampstead: Walter de la Mare and William Allingham (husband of watercolourist Helen Allingham). The book was perhaps intended to complement their by then famous brother's *Oxford Book of Verse* (1900). It may be considered an Edwardian canon of children's poetry for mothers and young children, and no doubt was a repository for the favourite poems of the three oldest Quiller-Couch offspring, who as bookish children in Bodmin had devoured the contents of their father's well-stocked library.

The years of family breakdown caused both Mabel and Q acute pain which lasted a lifetime. Writing offered a way of healing childhood traumas besides reliving childhood joys. Those of Mabel's stories I judge autobiographical include *The Carroll Girls* and *Kitty Trenire*, which both have as heroine a long-suffering elder sister who dutifully and lovingly takes on the role of 'mother' to her neglected siblings, at some cost to her own development – a familiar figure at all levels of Victorian society. *Kitty Trenire*, her best and longest book, depicts Kitty's father as a dreamy, unworldly GP and Kitty as his bookish elder daughter, trying to control a chaotic household of kindly, undisciplined servants with no mistress, the mother of the family having died. Q's description of his own father walking, his head in a book, behind a pony trap driven by his children coincides exactly with the portrait of Kitty's fictional father. Mabel's admiring description of Dan, Kitty's elder brother, is surely a portrait of Q as a boy. Perhaps that is why modest, shy Q nowhere comments on *Kitty Trenire* in any of his writings.

The Meanwells is a slighter tale; its dedication "to Lily in remembrance" is clearly a joke shared by the sisters. Here, the heroine is a little girl and the story's main event – when she misguidedly 'tidies' a field of newly planted turnips in a neighbour's garden, the result being attributed by the local people to Cornish 'pisgies' – no doubt reflects a real event.

Mabel's last 'autobiographical' novel was written in 1920. *A Cottage Rose* is interesting in that it reverses the conventional Rose Cottage which was the name of her maternal grandparents' home in Abbotskerswell, dear to the children as a place of order and care, rather different from the chaotic household in Bodmin. Significantly, the heroine is the mediator in a family row in which two branches are not on speaking terms. In 1921 Q was also thinking of their distant childhood when he took his own (grown-up) children to visit Rose Cottage, by now sadly neglected. *A Cottage Rose* is dedicated to 'Esther', the name of the worried elder sister who was the heroine of *The Carroll Girls* and possibly therefore a coded reference to her former self. All these books were written at 16 Downshire Hill, except for the last, which was written in an upstairs room at her sister's house, No.37. Mabel died there on 17 November 1924, and was buried in the northern extension of the graveyard at Hampstead parish church.

Photographs

Recently I found at the Camden Local Studies and Archives Centre a small photograph album filed under Quiller Couch, together with a letter from 'the Old Missis' to 'Florence' describing Mabel's funeral service conducted by the Vicar, Revd Mr Stocks. Florence was evidently too ill to attend herself. With the help of still living descendants of the family or their correspondents, especially Mrs Regina Glick of Leeds, who had conducted a long correspondence with Q's daughter Foy, all the people in the album were identified. The 'Old Missis' was in fact Lilian, and it may well have been she who put the album together as a memento of Mabel and of happy days in their Hampstead garden. The ailing Florence was

2 Mabel and (right) Lilian, professional photograph, possibly on the occasion of the publication of their jointly edited anthology of children's verse, 1911.

a much-loved family servant, perhaps the very one who had been with the family since the age of 8 and who celebrated her 50 years with the Quiller-Couches in a service at St Clement Danes attended by all the family, including those in Fowey. One can understand why family servants often feature in Mabel's stories for children: they were obviously a steadying influence when things in the family went wrong. Perhaps relatives of Florence gave her album to the local history library, but with no identification save the name Quiller-Couch.

All the small, amateurish photographs show scenes in the sunny back garden of No.37. Under one of them Lilian labels herself as the 'Old Missis'; her husband solemnly poses wearing a suit and Homburg hat in defiance of the sunshine. In another, her pet James the Scottie is submitting to being brushed by Lilian, who is kitted out with apron and white detachable sleeves to protect her frock There are two tabby cats, identified as Deborah and Bulgy, one of them labelled "The Real Missis". In the birthday picture dated 1920 already referred to (Fig 1) Mabel sits on a reclining chair, looking ill and rather worried about being photographed. Mabel is not photogenic, and must have been conscious of her plainness, with that 'lanky' hair piled high in dated Edwardian fashion and with the long upper lip evident in portraits of her brother. She looks older than her 56 years.

A larger photograph, separate from the album, is a professional portrait of the sisters, also in the garden against a striped awning (Fig 2). It seems commemorative, perhaps to celebrate the jointly edited anthology of children's verse in 1911. Although shown as an invalid, tucked up in a reclining chair, Mabel looks prettier and more in command of her appearance than in the 1920s. Several of the 1920s pictures show her sitting alone in the garden with her work basket, no doubt mending or doing 'useful plain sewing' for some charity bazaar. At her funeral the vicar referred to Mabel's 'lovely work' – whether referring to her children's books or useful plain sewing for charity is not clear – I hope he meant the former!

In 1915 their nephew Bevil, writing from the front in France, said "I'm so glad to hear the aunts in Hampstead have been visited by Zeppelins without causing apparently any alarm and despondency..." – the humorous tone evidently reflecting his pride in the aunts' calm in the face of danger. Bevil, the darling of the family, survived with honour right through the war, only to be struck down by influenza in February 1919. It was a devastating blow to all, and may be the reason the photographs a year later show Mabel looking so forlorn.

Q does not appear in the photographs, though he must often have visited Downshire Hill. Sadly, Mabel died 5 months before he opened Keats House in the adjoining street as a 'shrine to literature'. In his speech he complimented the Borough of Hampstead for its part in rescuing the house. Q was a prominent member of the National Committee which campaigned in the early 1920s to save the house from the bulldozers. With generous help from American supporters they had raised £4650, spent £3500 on repairs, and put the balance into an endowment fund. Those were the days!

Presumably Lilian and her lecturer husband were present, sadly missing Mabel. The Lobbans continued to live at 37 Downshire Hill until he retired in 1936, when they moved to Somerset, where they ended their days. The next resident of their 'little house' in Hampstead was Flora Robson, the celebrated actress.

Bibliography

F Brittan. *Arthur Quiller-Couch: A biographical study of Q.* CUP 1947
Charlotte Fyfe, ed. *The Tears of War: May Cannan & Bevil Quiller-Couch* Cavalier Books 2000
S C Roberts (ed.) *Memories and Opinions: An Unfinished Autobiography of Q.* CUP 1944
A L Rowse *Quiller Couch: A Portrait of 'Q'* Methuen 1988

Sources & acknowledgements

Thanks are due to Camden Local Studies & Archives Centre, Christopher Wade, Regina Glick, Elaine Moss, Guy Symondson, Michael Hammerson (for photographs).
An earlier version of this article was published in *Signal 84*, Approaches to Children's Books (Sep 1997) Thimble Press.

"Without parallel in the known world":
the chequered past of 277 Gray's Inn Road

by David Hayes

King's Cross today is a neighbourhood that many would choose to avoid. In the reign of George IV there were those who aspired to turn it into a fashionable resort[1]. Battle Bridge was renamed 'King's Cross', and a monument to the monarch was erected at the crossroads. The whole area around what is now Argyle Square was to have become a leisure complex called the Royal Panarmonion. Pleasure gardens, complete with a 'suspension railway', would have been surrounded by a hotel, theatre, ballroom and music academy. James Elmes, in his *Metropolitan Improvements* (1829), proclaimed that the removal of the turnpike gates from the New Road[2] would "render this part of the metropolis a principal object of attraction with the fashionable world". Such aspirations were unlikely to be realised in a district stigmatised by the presence (on the present King's Cross Station site) of London's smallpox and fever hospitals. The grandiose Panarmonion scheme was still unfinished when abandoned in 1832. Less spectacularly unsuccessful was a contemporary, lesser-known scheme on a site immediately to the east.

'Horse Bazaar'

The North London Horse & Carriage Repository (Fig 1) was bounded on the south by Manchester (now Argyle) Street; on the north by Derby (now St Chad's) Street; on the west by Liverpool (later Birkenhead) Street[3]; and on the east by Chichester Place (part of Gray's Inn Road). The impressive classical edifice was eventually tucked away behind the terraces of ordinary houses gradually built around it.

Elmes describes the building as "a noble structure of quadrangular form with a spacious arena in the centre". There are "stalls and looseboxes for about 200 horses" and "galleries for more than double that number of carriages". "The south front comprises a spacious mansion, the principal story in which is wholly occupied by one grand room". A later source[4] informs us that this "9-roomed house" is accessed from the west side and known as 12 Liverpool Street. At the north end, the upper storey comprises a "lofty ballroom, 100ft long, with 'orchestra'; approached by a noble flight of stairs, with a spacious landing; water and coal closets".

The premises had three named points of access. A 'City entrance' on Gray's Inn Road comprised a tetrastyle Ionic portico with two arched side-openings; numbered 16B Chichester Place, it became 277 Gray's Inn Road in 1862. A 'Grand entrance' in Derby Street, also porticoed, was fronted by a "large square plot of ground", and offered access for carriages through folding coach-doors. The 'Royal entrance' in Liverpool Street opened westward onto what should have been the Panarmonion gardens.

The building's architect was John Parkinson, 'of Pentonville'[5]. The precise date of its construction is uncertain, but the site was let on a 99-year lease dating from Christmas 1826[6]. Building was presumably in progress by 20

---

1 The Horse & Carriage Repository: 'north-west view' towards the assembly rooms and Derby Street entrance (T H Shepherd, 1828).

September 1827, when the Battle Bridge Paving Board met in special session to discuss it. Permission to erect a portico in Chichester Place as an entrance to the repository was granted; the lowering of the entrance by one foot was disallowed. A year later, the erection of the Derby Street portico was similarly debated. The horse repository is depicted in two prints dated October 1828 by T H Shepherd, but makes its first rate-book appearance only in January 1829.

The proprietor was one William Bromley of Euston Square[7]. His intended business was presumably modelled on earlier, similarly named concerns. The better-known Aldridge's Horse & Carriage

2 Robert Owen, pictured in 'Great Thoughts' (26 Aug 1893).

Repository was founded in 1776 and stood in Upper St Martin's Lane[8]. It specialised in the sale by auction of carriages and horses. Like Bromley's enterprise, Aldridge's was known popularly as a 'horse bazaar'; and there too carriages were housed in galleries[9].

It is unclear whether Bromley's repository ever really took off. Elmes reported that in the grand room of the mansion, "... by the gratuitous permission of the spirited proprietor ... some benevolent ladies lately held a bazaar, for the benefit of the Spanish Refugees"[10], which was attended by "upwards of 1,000 persons". As evidence of an equine presence we have only Shepherd's prints (possibly only an artist's impression); and an extravagant statement by Elmes that here there was a "greater regard ... to the *health* of that *invaluable animal* ... than in any other public establishment in the British Empire".

If the repository did ever function as intended, it seemingly never flourished. Bromley frequently attended meetings of the Battle Bridge Paving Board, the *ad hoc* body then responsible for paving and lighting the Battle Bridge estate. The Board met regularly, usually in the Globe alehouse at 11 Derby Street. At a meeting in June 1828, Bromley was among the 21 'inhabitant householders' sworn in as paving commissioners[11]. The rates payable on the horse repository were a recurrent agenda item at Board meetings, when Bromley was invariably present to plead for a reduction. A rateable value of £800, which was originally agreed, had been reduced to £250 when the repository first featured in the Poor Rate books of January 1829. Nine months later, Bromley secured agreement that his rates would be further reduced by a half.

'Toy Bazaar'

He was shortly to relaunch his enterprise as the Royal London Bazaar (RLB). On 6 December, the *Weekly Dispatch* announced that "A New Bazaar will be opened under Royal patronage[12] at the Carriage Repository, Gray's Inn Road, on a more magnificent plan than was ever witnessed in this country. Applications for the counters or Le Boutiques [sic] to be made to Mr Bromley, No.1 Euston Square; or to Mr Grainge at the Respository, if by letter post-free". A contemporary guidebook described the RLB as a 'Toy Bazaar', the word 'toy' used here in the sense of 'novelty'. The first public function at the RLB was the exhibition of a "panoramic picture in needlework of 1200 sq ft", "a most astonishing effort of female genius, the incessant labour of five years".

If the revamped bazaar enjoyed any success, it must have been seasonal. The January rate-books in both 1830 and 1831 show the premises as "empty". By June 1831 Bromley was behind with his rate payments, and asked for his arrears to be "converted into a debt by Deed of Assignment", a proposal rejected by the Paving Board. A month later he was back again with a further plea – the building, he claimed, has been "unoccupied for the most part during the previous year". The Board now relieved him of payment for the remaining half-year.

No formal link can be identified between the RLB and the neighbouring Panarmonion scheme, but they were clearly associated in the public mind. Elmes, in his early account of the horse bazaar, had remarked on "the large field ... adjoining hereto" which was "about to be converted into a handsome square and gardens, à la Tivoli". The offices of the Panarmonion Company were at 11 Liverpool Street, next door to the RLB 'mansion' at No.12; and in 1830 the two concerns mounted what we might call a joint promotion. An advertisement exclaimed that "Kings Cross! The Panarmonion Gardens! and the Royal London Bazaar, Liverpool Street, New Road — certainly the most splendid bazaar in Europe — are producing a magical effect in Metropolitan Improvements". In 1832, however, the Panarmonion project collapsed; two of its main promoters[13] were declared bankrupt. In February the press announced a sale of redundant bricks, stone and flint from the partly completed garden enclosure. Bromley was left isolated.

Owenite Institution

Living locally meanwhile, at 4 Crescent Place (now Burton Place), was the sexagenarian Welsh reformer Robert Owen (Fig 2), devoted at this time to the numerous co-operative institutions springing up under his influence. His Sunday 'social festivals' (or political lectures) aroused adverse comment wherever he went, forcing repeated changes of venue, from the Mechanics' Institution in Southampton Buildings (Holborn), to the Sans Souci Institution in Leicester Square, to the Burton Street Hall. At this former Baptist chapel, adjoining Owen's Crescent Place home, the London Co-operative Society had been founded in 1824.

On 12 December 1831 Owen addressed 1500 people at a public meeting in the RLB assembly room. Its purpose was to initiate an 'Association of the Intelligent & Well Disposed of the Working Classes to Remove the Causes of Poverty & Ignorance'. Owen proposed as chairman one George Evans Bruce. Dr Birkbeck and Rowland Hill were among those appointed as directors of the mercifully renamed 'Society to Remove the Causes of Poverty & Ignorance'. The RLB would serve as its 'Institution'. Nine days earlier William Bromley had written to Owen, expressing a wish to promote the "amelioration of the wretched conditions of the working classes of all sects and denominations". He offered the proposed society free use of the RLB "without any emolument on [his] account", provided only that affairs were managed personally by Owen, and that he received "fair remuneration ... when circumstances permit". A time limit appears to have been later imposed on the offer: Owen would have the option of purchasing the building at the end of 1832. He did, in fact, pay Bromley 6 months' ground rent and £700 towards the fixtures in the hall.

Owen now used the assembly room for his monthly 'social festivals'. *The Crisis*, a weekly penny paper which Owen edited[14], was adorned with vignettes depicting the RLB. On 22 September 1832, the *Poor Man's Guardian* reported a debate held there between the Owenites and the National Political Union on the relative merits of co-operation and political rights.

The stated objectives of Owen's Institution were tenfold. They included:

- Staging weekly lectures, and establishing a library and reading-room;
- Founding "seminaries ... for young persons of all ages and both sexes", and "schools of industry to train the young in all the arts of life";
- Preparing food, "in the best and most economical manner, for the inmates of the institution and the inhabitants of the surrounding district";
- Receiving "provisions and clothing ... to be exchanged through the medium of labour notes" (see later); and opening a bank "in which to exchange the labour notes for the currency of the country";
- Procuring land "near the banks of the Regent's Canal", a "healthy" spot where the young would be trained in gardening, horticulture and farming — while incidentally providing a supply of fresh vegetables for the Institution.

It is unclear how many of these aims were achieved during its year-long existence in Gray's Inn Road, soon to end abruptly, as we shall see.

Irvingite Chapel

For several months in 1832, Owen shared 16B with an unlikely bedfellow. Edward Irving[15] was the charismatic minister of the Caledonian (or National Scotch) Church in nearby Regent Square. Always controversial were his prophecies of the Second Coming, and his unorthodox style of worship which encouraged 'speaking in tongues'. It was, however, his avowed belief in the sinfulness of Christ's nature that led to charges of heresy, and his expulsion from Regent Square by the Presbytery. On Sunday 6 May 1832, the Revd Irving and 800 loyal members of his congregation took refuge at the RLB, some of whose first-floor rooms became their temporary chapel. They did not stay for long. Irving disliked being associated with the materialistic, and allegedly atheistic, Owen. In the autumn he and his flock moved on, to Benjamin West's picture gallery in Newman Street (Fitzrovia)[16].

'Labour Exchange'

Meanwhile, in September, Owen had opened at the RLB his National Equitable Labour Exchange (NELE). Similar institutions already existed locally, not labour exchanges in the 20th-century sense, but places of trade where poor artisans could sell their produce at a fair price[17]. Two years previously, an Exchange Bazaar had been founded in Hatton Garden by the British Association for Promoting Co-operative Knowledge. A 'Labour Exchange' was launched in early 1832 by one William King at the Gothic Hall, New Road, Marylebone. Lesser establishments existed in both Tottenham Court Road and Red Lion Square.

The opening of Owen's NELE on Monday 17 September caused severe traffic congestion in Gray's Inn Road, and on the Thursday the Exchange was forced to close for several days while merchandise was classified and valued. Goods were valued in a currency based on the cost of materials and the number of work-hours involved in their production, less a penny in the shilling as commission. Articles were deposited in exchange for 'labour notes'[18]. These notes

gained quite widespread acceptance, being honoured by many ordinary tradesmen, by several theatres, and at the tollgate on Waterloo Bridge.

The NELE was at first a great success. In the first week, deposits totalled almost £10,000. In the space of 17 weeks, they amounted to 445,501 hours, and exchanges to 376,166 hours, leaving a balance 69,335 hours, or £1,733/7/6 in real money. Tailors, cabinet-makers and shoemakers were the chief depositors.

Owen evicted

At the end of 1832 Owen's brief tenure ended suddenly, when Bromley called 'time' on the no-rent agreement. He demanded that Owen either purchase the RLB outright (for £17,000), or pay rent of £1,400 with ground rent of £320. A public meeting at the RLB was informed that the Institution could not afford such expense[19].

The Owenites were then promptly evicted. According to the notoriously partisan Holyoake, they were physically ejected by a band of hired thugs[20]. Most accounts of this episode paint Bromley as the villain of the piece. Holyoake claims that Bromley "saw money-earning powers in the undertaking and schemed to come into possession". The more objective Podmore concedes that he was probably genuinely sympathetic to Owen's aims, but obliged to exact payment because of his own financial embarrassment. It was "not that Bromley was unfairly smart, but that Owen was marvellously negligent".

The business of the NELE was briefly transferred to the Rotunda in Blackfriars Road, where a South London branch had been started a few weeks earlier. In May 1833, the parent exchange reopened at 14 Charlotte Street (Fitzrovia)[21]. In July it was sold to the United Trades Association, under whose auspices it failed in the following year. One reason for its eventual failure may have been that the valuation of goods was not an exact science. Some artisans spent longer completing an article than others. Some goods were therefore under-priced and others over-priced. Buyers inevitably bought the cheaper merchan-

3   Exhibition advertisement of ?1834 (Heal Collection).

The Grand Mechanical and beautifully Picturesque Exhibition being received with the highest marks of approbation and astonishment to every beholder, will be repeated every evening at Eight and in the Day time at Half-past Two o'Clock precisely.

ROYAL LONDON BAZAAR,

Gray's Inn Road, and Liverpool Street, New Road,

IS OPEN TWICE EACH DAY.

MR. MILLER'S GRAND MECHANICAL AND PICTURESQUE

Exhibition of Arts!!

This Exhibition is composed of beautiful representations of celebrated CITIES, SHIPPING, &c. Exhibiting to the Eye the wonderful combined powers of Mechanism and Painting.—The Exhibition without the aid of any Optical Illusion presents to the mind of the Spectator the extraordinary effects resulting from Mechanism, and affords an animated display of picturesque Scenery.—The Proprietor begs to inform the Public that it is not Transparency or a Flat Picture, but a real

Imitation of Nature!

Each Piece is animated by a variety of Figures, Carriages, Horses, and other Animals, &c.

PIECE I.—THE CITY OF

CONSTANTINOPLE,

WITH THE SUBURBS OF PERA AND GALATA,

The Spectator is here presented with a beautiful representation of the noble City of Constantinople. To the right of the City is seen the Sea of Marmora, and to the left the Black Sea, which divides Europe from Asia. Among the various Mosques in the extreme distance will be distinguished from its lofty and noble Dome, that of Sancta Sophia, a Greek Church, dedicated to the Holy Wisdom ; and the Mosque of the Sultan Achmet, acknowledged by all Travellers to be one of the finest buildings ever raised by the Turks. The most prominent object in the View is the

SERAGLIO, or PALACE of the SULTAN.

The view will be enlivened by a number of Turkish Men of War, Barges and Ships of various Nations, appearing in motion, the procession of the Sultan leaving the Seraglio, attended by his numerous Officers. In the foreground will be seen a number of Camels, Oxen, &c. caparisoned in the Costume of the Country ; Turkish Cavalry and Infantry, with various other figures too numerous to mention

PIECE II.—THE

CITY OF FLORENCE.

In this Scene various Craft on the River appear in motion ; Swans and other aquatic Fowl are seen on the Water, feeding, fluttering their wings, diving, &c. On the Land and across the Bridge, innumerable Figures are seen, so that the Spectator is almost induced to believe that he is viewing the effects of Nature rather than the work of Art.—Also a beautiful representation of an Aquatic Exhibition.

PIECE III.—A SPLENDID REPRESENTATION OF

His Majesty Landing in Scotland.

Embracing an extensive view of the Scottish Metropolis and surrounding Country, including Arthur's Seat, Salisbury Craigs, the Calton Hill, Castle, &c. In this Scene will appear a number of Steam Vessels, Shipping, and small Craft, Commodore O'Brien who sailed from the West of Ireland, to whom His Majesty gave ten Sovereigns, a Figure walking on the Water after the manner of Mr. Kent, the Squadron firing a Royal Salute. It is impossible to describe this sublime spectacle so as to convey to the mind an adequate idea of its interesting effect.

A VARIETY OF CHINESE ARTIFICIAL

FIRE WORKS,

Consisting of 1, Piece of Architecture in the City of Rome,—2, The Garden of Flora, 3, Grand Roman Temple—4, Chinese Pagoda Bridge—5, Grand Persian Temple—6, The Temple of Fame—7, Homage to England.———To conclude with a

STORM AT SEA!

With all the Phenomena of an agitated Ocean ! Clouds that obscure the Sky ! rain falling in torrents ! lightning ! thunder ! &c. A vessel beating against the Tempest struck by a Thunder-bolt, and engulphed in the waves ! Together with the miraculous escape of a distressed Seaman to a neighbouring rock. Brave exertions of the Crew of a Life-boat, who rescue the exhausted mariners from impending destruction.

BOXES 2s. PIT 1s. GALLERY 6d. Children under 12 with Parties Half-price to the Boxes.
In order to accommodate Juvenile Parties, there will be an Exhibition every day at Half-past Two o'Clock
EVENING DOORS OPEN AT HALF PAST SEVEN & TO COMMENCE AT EIGHT Precisely.

₊ Parties wishing to have a Private View, by giving One Day's Notice to Mr. Miller, at the THEATRE OF ARTS, may be Accommodated.

dise, leaving the Exchange with many unsaleable, higher-valued items on its hands.

Robert Owen's eviction from the RLB did not end his association with Chichester Place. Until 1834 he remained the ratepayer at No.15, a house (owned by Flanders) which he had apparently rented while still living in Crescent Place.

Bromley, meanwhile, had joined forces with one of Owen's colleagues, a Mr McConnell. Together they formed the National Land[22] & Equitable Labour Exchange Company, which tried to continue the Gray's Inn Road business as a private venture, opening for deposits on 21 January 1833. Employees of the exchange were now paid in cash to prevent their "trafficking in the Notes or stores of the Exchange for goods deposited therein". An advertising placard confessed that "a few stands in the Provisions Department are disengaged". This may have been an understatement: Bromley and McConnell apparently met with little success, and by August 1833 the rate-books once again showed an "empty" building.

Bromley then resurrected his Royal London Bazaar. An upbeat advertisement of 1834 declared that here you might "... purchase any of the thousand & 1 varieties of fancy & useful articles; or you could lounge an agreeable hour either in the Promenades, or in the Exhibitions that are wholly without parallel in the known world!" Fig 3 gives a taste of the kind of attractions on offer. A further "great draw" was the 'Waterloo Carriage', the coach in which Napoleon had fled from the battlefield at Waterloo, and which in 1834 had "found its way to a horse repository in Gray's Inn Road"[23]. It remained there for several years, until purchased in 1842 by Madame Tussaud's.

Waxworks

Marie Tussaud (Fig 4), the Swiss wax-modeller (b.1761), came to London in 1802, with her 4-year-old son Joseph. In post-revolutionary Paris, she had attended the guillotine to make death masks of its victims. Unhappy with Parisian life, she had separated from her ineffectual husband François, leaving him to run the Paris waxworks, and intent on a new life in England. Her first London exhibition was mounted in Drury Lane. For some 26 years Marie toured Britain with her portable show, exhibiting in England, Scotland and Ireland. A tour of southern England in 1833 ended in Kent at the Green Man assembly rooms on Blackheath Hill.

Thereafter she settled permanently in London, and it was to the RLB that she first came, arriving in December and opening her 'Exhibition & Promenade' in January 1834. Opening hours were 11-4 and 7-10. Admission cost a shilling; children paid sixpence, and special half-price evening sessions were laid on 'for the poor'. A life-sized waxwork of Marie herself stood at the top of the stairs, as if to welcome visitors. At opposite ends of the assembly room were her two main tableaux, depicting the coronations of Napoleon and of William IV. Marie's sons Joseph and Francis[24] organised and played in the orchestra, which performed twice daily at 2 o'clock and 7.30. For sixpence extra one could enter a Second Room, "inadvisable for ladies to visit", where the death masks of guillotine victims and murderers (including Burke and Hare) were displayed — a precursor of the Chamber of Horrors. Among the show's patrons in 1834 were the Princess Augusta and Prince George; for once, at least, the 'Royal entrance' must have justified its name.

In June the Tussauds left Gray's Inn Road for a 6-month local tour, exhibiting firstly at the Lowther Arcade off the Strand, then in Camberwell and Hackney. Elaborate preparations were meanwhile in hand for a triumphal return to the RLB at Christmas. The assembly room was transformed into a 'Grand Corinthian Saloon': 2000 sq ft of 'glorious' gilding was supplied by Mr Syffert of Great Queen Street at a cost of over £1,000, and papier-mâché ornamentation was by Mr Bielefeld of the New Road. The tableaux were as previously, with the addition of an effigy of the popular Duke of Sussex. On 29 December the exhibition reopened. Marie may well have intended to remain permanently in Gray's Inn Road, so that Madame Tussaud's might today have been a Camden tourist attraction. But in March 1835 the RLB was needed for other purposes, and the waxworks was forced to move on, to the Baker Street Bazaar[25].

4   Madame Tussaud in 1838 (Heal Collection).

Bromley bows out

Twelve months earlier, and despite Marie Tussaud's "decided success", Bromley had cut his losses and sold the premises over her head. On 3 March 1834 the RLB was "peremptorily" auctioned at Garraway's Coffee House on Cornhill, "under circumstances that will preclude any reservation". The particulars of sale describe the principal storey as comprising "3 splendid capacious corridors on 3 sides of a quadrangle" with "iron balconies affording a pleasant promenade". On the ground floor, the stables have become a "range of store rooms or warehouses 15-feet high". Reference is made to a colonnade of "massive iron columns". These were curiously absent from the earlier Shepherd prints, indicative maybe of some licence on the artist's part. The building was now advertised as being adaptable to any number of different purposes, from a National School or hospital to an "amphitheatre" or railway warehouse. Included in the auction lot were two adjacent houses, evidently owned by Bromley, at 17-18 Chichester Place.

Presiding at the sale was Bromley himself, which suggests that auctioneering was indeed his true vocation. By August 1833 he had vacated his fine town-house on the west side of Euston Square. His address was now given as "Saville [i.e. Savile] House, Leicester Square". This former mansion, on the Empire cinema site, was by then multiply-occupied and housed a wondrous assortment of entertainments, astronomical, mechanical and picturesque[26].

After Bromley

Under new ownership, 16B Chichester Place settled down to a more humdrum existence as a goods repository and furniture pantechnicon run by William Lightfoot and Martin Stuteley. During the 'Railway Mania', surveyors and draughtsmen worked in part of the building on various, usually abortive, railway projects. By the 1850s the premises had been renumbered 16½ and, under Edward Reeder Stuteley, named the North London Depository for Goods. Then living in the 'mansion' at 12 Liverpool Street was one Neville Alfred Hooper, a manufacturer of "patent lentils" and probably the "quack doctor" who, according to Abrahams, traded at the RLB as the 'Palace of Hygiene'[27]. In the following decade, the old assembly rooms became the 800-seat St George's Hall, and was used for panoramas, 'private theatricals', promenade concerts and evangelistic sermons. The rest of the building was occupied by the London Depository Company, and used also by the brewers William Mark & Co. and "British wine makers" Whitwell & Mark.

In 1872 the premises became the bottling store of Whitbread's, managed initially by their bottled-beer agent Robert Baker. By 1890, the brewery had substantially rebuilt the old bazaar, roofing over the arena and installing wooden galleries for the storage of bottled ale. The 'City entrance' was remodelled to improve vehicular access. Its Ionic columns were dismantled, and the façade was adorned with two large three-dimensional beer bottles. The north side-entrance was removed. Attempts by the company to dispose of the property in 1905 (for £33,000) were unsuccessful, and Whitbread's were still listed as in occupation over half a century later.

The building has subsequently become an oily haunt of motor mechanics, serving *inter alia* as a servicing depot for Jaguar cars; the up-market carriages deposited there today are horseless. The mutilated 'City entrance' survives at 277 Gray's Inn Road, and is Grade-II Listed.

Notes

1 See *Camden History Review* 17, pp13-16.
2 Now Marylebone, Euston and Pentonville Roads.
3 The section of Birkenhead Street to the south of St Chad's Street is now closed, lying within security gates erected to protect the council flats of Riverfleet and neighbouring blocks.
4 Particulars of Sale, Garraway's, 1834 (Heal Collection).
5 Possibly related to Joseph Parkinson, the architect of Hunters Lodge in Belsize Lane, and a resident in 1825 of Cloudesley Square, Pentonville.
6 Messrs Flanders, Dunston and Robinson were ground landlords of the Battle Bridge estate, which they had acquired by Act of Parliament in 1824. William Flanders owned many of the houses surrounding the bazaar, and may well have been the lessor.
7 Apparently not identical with the line engraver William Bromley who lived locally at 29 Burton Street in 1813-18, and later in Fitzroy Square.
8 Just in Westminster, on the site of Orion House.
9 Illustrated in Richardson, p.337. Horse sales continued at Aldridge's until 1926. The firm moved in 1940 to William Road (off Hampstead Road), where it specialised in the auction of motor-cars and greyhounds.
10 Many of the refugees had settled in nearby Somers Town (see *Camden History Review* 6).
11 Others included Dunston, Flanders and Robinson; and Charles Inwood, a member of the well-known local family of architects.
12 The patronage of George IV was easily obtained for any scheme which might enhance the metropolitan environment.
13 Architect Stephen Geary, and company secretary Francis Guynette.
14 It was later edited by his son, Robert Dale Owen, until it folded in 1834.
15 Then living at 13 Judd Place East, New Road (now the St Pancras Station frontage).
16 Breaking finally with the Church of Scotland in 1833 (a year before his death), Irving founded there a new communion – the Catholic Apostolic (or Irvingite) Church – for which the Church of Christ the King (Gordon Square) was eventually erected in 1851-54.
17 "Agriculturalists, Gardeners, Manufacturers, provision merchants, warehousemen, wholesale and retail dealers of all descriptions, mechanics, and all others who may be inclined to dispose of their various articles of trade and merchandise in the only equitable manner in which men can mutually dispose of their property to each other – viz., its value in labour for equal value in labour, without the intervention of money – are requested to communicate with Mr Samuel Austin at the Equitable Labour Exchange. All letters must be post-paid. ROBERT OWEN" (*The Crisis*, June 1832).
18 See illustration in CHS *Newsletter* 141.
19 "At a public meeting held on Monday afternoon in the lecture-room of the Working Classes in Gray's Inn Road, the Rev. Dr Wade in the chair, Mr Owen announced that without liberal public donations the association could not be carried on upon the same premises another year, the rental being £1,400 per annum" (*John Bull*, 13 January 1833).
20 "Mr Bromley was so impatient of re-possession that he did not wait even for their leaving, but procured a mob of men and broke into the place, and let in sixty-four ruffians, who smashed the secretary's doors in, took possession of the fixtures belonging to the Exchange, and turned the directors into the street".
21 Not number 4, as several writers have asserted. Holyoake describes the Charlotte Street building as some 250 feet long, running through to a rear entrance in John (now Whitfield) Street. In the middle it opened out into a large rectangular space with galleries. This description exactly matches the premises shown on the Ordnance Survey map of 1870 as the 'Oxford Pantechnicon', though listed in Kelly's as the 'Bedford Pantechnicon'. 40 years earlier its front entrance was at 14 Charlotte Street (still earlier home to Charles Dibdin, the dramatist and song-writer). The "back premises", at 93 John Street, were built on the site of a brewery (Thomson's map of 1803). The rate-book of January 1834 shows at both addresses an "Institution of the Industrious Classes" (ratepayer, Jacob Dixon). The Charlotte Street entrance was later decommissioned, so that when the Owenite Scientific & Literary Institution was opened here in 1840, it was described as "in John Street". 14 Charlotte Street, renumbered 30, is now the Étoile restaurant. 93 John Street (later 19 Whitfield Street) vanished after wartime damage, and its site is occupied by the Crabtree Fields open space.
22 According to Abrahams, the 'Land' in the title related to a "quasi-socialistic-local-colonization undertaking known as the Experimental Gardens". It involved the leasing of plots "at convenient distances from the metropolis, or on the land of the intended railroad from Birmingham to King's Cross [sic]". Edwardian research into this enterprise had yielded only "fragmentary results".
23 First exhibited in England at the Egyptian Hall, Piccadilly, it later toured the country, earning its owner, William Bullock, £35,000 in admission fees, before finding a home at the RLB. (Information supplied to Abrahams by Mr John T Tussaud.)
24 A baby in 1802, and left with his father in Paris, Francis had joined Marie in Britain during her touring years.
25 In the former King Street Barracks, near Portman Square. In 1885 the waxworks moved on again to its present site in Marylebone Road.
26 See Tames, pp.25-29. Efforts to identify Bromley with any of these separately run establishments, or to trace his later movements, have proved fruitless.
27 Abrahams, p.134. King's Cross was noted for its purveyors of patent remedies; *cf.* the College of Health (*East of Bloomsbury*, p77), and Cabburn's Dispensary (*Camden History Review* 23, pp13-15).

Sources

Battle Bridge Paving Board: minutes, 1827-33
Goad's insurance plan, 1890
Heal Collection, C IV 64-72
Kelly's *Post Office London directory*, 1863-
St Pancras Vestry: Poor Rate, 1826-49

Abrahams, Aleck "No.277 Gray's Inn Road", *The Antiquary* April 1908 : 128-134
Camden History Society *Newsletter* 141 (Jan 1994)
Cole, G D H *The Life of Robert Owen*. 3rd ed. (Cass, 1965), pp262-266
Elmes, James *Metropolitan Improvements* (Jones & Co., 1829)
Hair, John *Regent Square: 80 Years of a London Congregation* (James Nisbet, 1899)
Holyoake, G J *The History of Co-operation in England* (Trübner, 1875-9)
Leon, Robert "The man who made King's Cross", *Camden History Review* 1992 ; 17 : 13-16
Leslie, Anita *Madame Tussaud, Waxworker Extraordinary* (Hutchinson, 1978)
Podmore, Frank *Robert Owen: a Biography* (Hutchinson, 1906)
Richardson, John *The Annals of London* (Cassell, 2000)
Survey of London, Vol.24 *King's Cross and Neighbourhood* (LCC, 1952), pp111-112
Tames, Richard *Soho Past* (Historical Publications, 1994)

David Hayes, a chartered librarian, is Associate Editor of this *Review*. His interest in 277 Gray's Inn Road was aroused while researching the CHS book *East of Bloomsbury*, which he compiled.

Bollards in Camden

by A D Harvey

There are older bollards in Southwark - notably the muzzles of two 18th-century 24-pounder cannon protruding from the pavement at the junction of Borough High Street and Union Street, which appear to be several decades earlier than the ship's guns (probably 6- and 12-pounders) in Cannon Lane and Cannon Place in Hampstead (Fig 1) - and more dignified bollards in the City of Westminster, including some with the monograms of George IV and William IV in Waterloo Place; but the bollards of Camden illustrate the vagaries of London local government more strikingly than those of any other London borough.

The earliest examples seem to have been erected by landlords developing their estates during the post-Waterloo housing boom. There are two bollards marked

SOMMERS
TOWN
1817

in Phoenix Road, at the junctions with Ossulston Street and Chalton Street, and a similar bollard that has migrated - no doubt with the assistance of Council workmen - to the junction of Heath Street and Whitestone Lane in Hampstead (Fig 2); a couple of Foundling Estate bollards still *in situ* in Guilford Street; some unmarked bollards, probably a little later in date, decorated with vaguely gothic patterning, in the Kentish Town area (Fig 3); and two bollards embossed with what may have been miniature crests, at the junction of Hastings Street and Tonbridge Street, and in Drummond Crescent.

The earliest bollards proclaiming themselves to be municipal property are in Wakefield Mews and in Drummond Crescent: they are marked

ST P
S.W.D.
1826

(i.e. St Pancras Sanitary - or Street ? - or Surveyors ? - Works Department).

In Hampstead there are examples (Fig 4) in Perrin's Lane and Holly Hill marked

ST JOHN'S
HAMPSTEAD
E. GRIFFIN
&
J. KELLY
1828

(Griffin and Kelly being presumably the churchwardens), and one of similar design with the date 1836 in Hampstead Square at the junction with Heath Street. In Cheney Road, at the side of King's Cross Station, there is a row of bollards which bear the letters S.P.P. (St Pancras Parish) and the date 1854, and at the junction of Conway Street and Maple Street there is a single bollard marked

ST P
S.W.D.
1855

There is a similar bollard on the west (City of Westminster) side of Cleveland Street at the junction of Greenwell Street, and two of the same design but with the lettering partially erased in Warren Street, at the junction of Richardson Mews (Fig 5). A single bollard further along Warren Street marked S.P.A. and a similar specimen in Wakefield Mews may be of the same vintage, though whether the letters S.P. stand for St Pancras, and what the letter A. might signify, is uncertain: a bollard in Drummond Crescent marked with a crown and

IV
GR,

apparently abducted from the Regent Street area, testifies to how little the current positioning of bollards has to do with their original location.

1 Cannon Lane NW3

2 Heath Street/Whitestone Lane NW3

3 Anglers Lane NW5

4 Perrin's Lane NW3

From the mid-1850s onwards the Vestry of St Pancras began to make a name for itself as one of the most dynamic, progressive and big-spending of London's local authorities - a reputation taken even further by its successor, the Metropolitan Borough of St Pancras, after 1900. Today there appear to be more bollards in Camden than in any other part of London, and it sometimes seems that half of them date from after 1855 bearing the monogram (Fig 6)

$$S^T\ P$$
$$P.\ M$$

i.e. St Pancras Parish Middlesex. These bollards came in two basic patterns: one, very massive, with a square section, the other only half as thick. There are also a small number marked

$$S^T$$
$$P\ P$$
$$M$$

which appear to be slightly older; the stylised heraldic shield on which the letters are embossed has incurving sides whereas the others, like examples after 1890, have a shield with straight sides. In 1889 St Pancras ceased to be part of the County of Middlesex and became part of the County of London, and in 1900 it ceased to be a parish and became a metropolitan borough: but by 1889 there were already enough St Pancras Parish Middlesex bollards in existence to cater for all possible needs for the next 70 years, and one only very occasionally encounters bollards marked

$$S^T\ P$$
$$L$$

i.e. St Pancras London, or

$$S^T\ P$$
$$BC$$

i.e. St Pancras Borough Council, or simply

$$S^T\ P.$$

The other local authorities thrown together with St Pancras to make up the London Borough of Camden in 1965 were much more modest in their bollardeering. Though their populations were much smaller, Hampstead and Holborn were much richer *per capita* than St Pancras - in 1900 amongst the six richest London boroughs in terms of rateable value per head of population - but their civic leaders had little interest in lavish spending programmes. The only bollards marked as the property of the Vestry of St John's Hampstead are the few predating the reign of Queen Victoria, mentioned in my second paragraph; I am still looking for an example of *any* item of street furniture with the mark of the Metropolitan Borough of Hampstead. What appears to be a unique St G.D.B.W. bollard has migrated to Anglers Lane in Kentish Town (Fig 7): before 1900 St. George's District Board of Works was the local authority in the western half of what became the Metropolitan Borough of Holborn - and there is a bollard marked

$$HOLBORN$$
$$1937$$

in Emerald Street (Fig 8). It seems unlikely that Holborn ordered only a single bollard, but it cannot have been a very large batch as the rest seem to have vanished. Fortunately there were enough bollards marked with the St Pancras Parish Middlesex monogram to make up for any deficiency, and since the establishment of the London Borough of Camden numerous examples have been installed outside the original boundaries of St Pancras, notably round Hampstead Heath in the vicinity of the station at South End Green.

Dr A D Harvey was born and brought up in Colchester and studied at Oxford and Cambridge Universities, but has lived in London since 1977. His most recent book is *Arnhem* (Cassell 2001).

Photographs by A V Beedell.

Corrigenda

In the article by David Hayes on 'Holborn's Church of Humanity' (*Camden History Review* 24, pp 6–11), an unexplained computer fault led to the misprinting of several numerals.

On p 11, in Note 19, for "1802" read "1892".

In Note 24, for "men 29" read "men 28", and for "8 years" read "7 years".

The first Note 27 should be numbered 26.

In Note 27, for "1864" read "1854".

Under 'Other Sources: O.S. maps', for "1924" read "1914".

The author also wishes to confess to a human error in his 'Epilogue' (p 10). The concluding remarks should have read: "The house-numbering scheme [in Rugby Street] remained unaltered, with one exception: No.19 became No.20. Ever an anomaly, No.19 had been the only odd number on the street's otherwise even-numbered north side. The pre-war rationalisation would have pleased Comte's order-loving disciples at the Church of Humanity."

5 Warren Street/Richardson Mews W1

6 Windmill Street W1

7 Anglers Lane NW5

8 Emerald Street WC1

From stones to ohms:
The history of electricity in Hampstead and the Central Supply Station, Lithos Road

by Brian Cox & Bob Gilham, *edited by* Peter G Scott

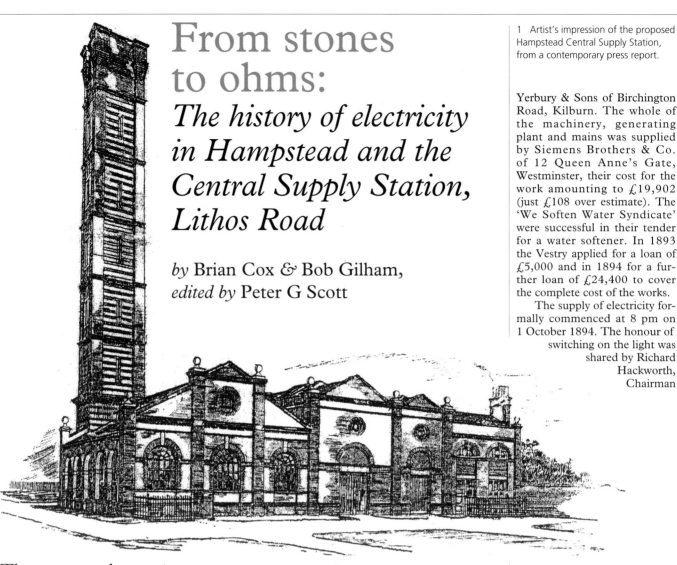

1 Artist's impression of the proposed Hampstead Central Supply Station, from a contemporary press report.

The stoneyard that became Lithos Road

On 23 July 1880, the Vestry of the Parish of St John, Hampstead bought a plot of land from Sir Spencer Maryon Wilson for £4000. The land had already changed hands a number of times: there are 18 entries on the conveyance from the first entry on 21 December 1829.

Sir Spencer stipulated that the Vestry "...will not use the said land hereinbefore expressed to be hereby granted for Hospital or Mortuary purposes or for the deposit of mud or for any purpose which might cause any nuisance to the said Sir Spencer Maryon Wilson...". One of the conditions of the sale was that the Vestry of St John "...should construct and for ever thereafter maintain a good and sufficient road forty feet wide to a point on the Finchley Road...".

The land consisted of a triangular plot between the Midland Railway and the London & North-Western (Hampstead Junction) Railway. The three sides of the plot measured 594, 595, and 284 feet. The Vestry allocated another £4000 for the construction of two brick walls 595 and 284 feet long, the building of a dwelling for staff accommodation (always known as 'The Cottage'), a carpenter's workshop and stables, and for equipping the yard for stonecutting. The two brick walls still form a boundary to the site. The Vestry used the site for over 10 years as a stone yard (the Greek for stone is *lithos*).

Electric beginnings

In the year the Vestry acquired the land, Joseph Swan in England and Thomas Edison in America invented the electric lamp with an incandescent carbon filament. Four years later Sir Charles Parsons invented the steam turbine.

In 1890 the Vestry resolved that setting up an undertaking to supply electric light should be prepared by an expert. W H Preece, CB, FRS (later Sir William Preece) was appointed consulting engineer, and his report and scheme were duly presented to the Vestry, who then applied to the Board of Trade for a Provisional Order.

The Hampstead Vestry electricity undertaking came into being on 27 June 1892, when the Electric Lighting Orders Confirmation (No.6) Act 1892 received the Royal Assent. It was only the second municipal electric light undertaking to be formed, the first being at neighbouring St Pancras. Construction of the Central Supply Station began in 1893, but the foundation stone was not laid until 23 May 1894, when a dinner was held at the Midland Grand Hotel, St Pancras.

The Central Supply Station

The buildings of the Central Supply Station (Fig 1) were erected in the stoneyard at a cost of £9,052 11s 6d (£1,702 11s 6d over estimate) by Yerbury & Sons of Birchington Road, Kilburn. The whole of the machinery, generating plant and mains was supplied by Siemens Brothers & Co. of 12 Queen Anne's Gate, Westminster, their cost for the work amounting to £19,902 (just £108 over estimate). The 'We Soften Water Syndicate' were successful in their tender for a water softener. In 1893 the Vestry applied for a loan of £5,000 and in 1894 for a further loan of £24,400 to cover the complete cost of the works.

The supply of electricity formally commenced at 8 pm on 1 October 1894. The honour of switching on the light was shared by Richard Hackworth, Chairman of the Vestry of St John, Hampstead, and James Thwaites, Chairman of the Electric Lighting Committee. The former switched on the supply to the underground cables which had been laid in Finchley Road from Arkwright Road to Swiss Cottage. Here, 22 arc lights had been erected for public lighting.

Hampstead vs St Pancras

A contemporary account of the inauguration of the supply states: "There is some difference between the system adopted in Hampstead and that used in St Pancras parish and by the Electric Battery Company, which has supplied a good many of the private residences.[1] In the neighbouring parish the low tension system is used, but this can only serve a limited area, and has already necessitated our neighbours building another station. By this system, however, the electric power can be stored [in batteries], and in consequence the machinery does not run at night. In Hampstead it has been considered advisable to adopt the high tension system, which allows for the providing of a larger area; but this...requires constant service, as any cessation of the engines [the steam engines driving the dynamos] means the cutting off of the supply."

The Central Supply Station at Hampstead fed the high-tension cable network at 2,000 volts, alternating current, single phase. For domestic supplies this was transformed down to 105/210 volts by underground transformer chambers at street corners.[2]

The rates of pay prevailing at that time are of interest. Richard Alexander Chattock, AMIEE (who later became City Electrical Engineer of Birmingham) was appointed Chief Engineer at a salary of £200 per annum. The entire staff required for operating the plant at the station and to maintain distribution mains consisted of three assistant engineers (Fig 2), three drivers, three firemen, three regulators, two trimmers, a fitter, two labourers, an engine cleaner, a wireman, a lamp trimmer, a storekeeper and a clerk. Their combined weekly wages amounted to £32 14s 11d.

Growth

The original generating capacity totalled only 625 kW. The number of units sold in the first 15 months from the commencement of supply to the end of the year 1895 was 192,528; the maximum demand was 241 kW, and the number of consumers connected was 246.

From a Vestry report dated 1895/6 it is noted that "the Electric Light Undertaking of the Vestry has passed its initial stage. Its growth has far exceeded even the most sanguine expectations".

Number of consumers
Christmas 1894   47
Ladyday 1895   74
Midsummer Day 1895   116
Michaelmas Day 1895   158
Christmas 1895   246
Ladyday 1896   305

It is also recorded that an operating loss of £2,916 was sustained. Fig 3 gives an idea of the size of the machinery used for the operation.

The Vestry report of 1896/7 for the "Central Supply Station, Stoneyard, Lithos Road" disclosed: "Our coal bill for the previous year was very big, in fact one of the highest in the kingdom, resulting in the 'Automatic Stokers' being thrown out, and a new contract for the best 'Welsh Smokeless' coal being contracted."

Later Vestry reports state that the station consumed 10 tons of coal a day, one man having to shovel 5 tons a day. The weekly coal train was brought into the site via a siding from the London & North-Western Railway which crossed the public footpath (West End Lane to Finchley Road). This operation normally took half an hour, so while the gates were closed across the footpath the public walked through the generating station via a small wicket gate. The station's chimney, 240 feet high, was often accused of belching black smoke over Hampstead due to the burning of indifferent coal.

Necessary expansion

The Vestry minutes record that during the winter of 1897 the consumers experienced their first load-shedding, the reason given being shortage of plant. The Vestry realised that the generating capacity of the station was inadequate, and plans were drawn up for an extension.

The extension was constructed in 1900/1. A 581-ft well was sunk for water, and a second well, 400 ft deep, was later drilled. The generating capacity was increased to 2,056 kW and the number of consumers now totalled 2,060. The workforce increased in size accordingly, and began to organise its social life as well (Fig 4) – something which continues to this day.

At the outbreak of war in 1914 the total plant capacity had risen to 5,884 kW and the number of consumers to 8,121. No new plant was installed during WW I or after. In 1920, when the number of consumers totalled 10,047, the Chief Electrical Engineer & Manager wrote to the Mayor and Aldermen of Hampstead: "Some of the boilers, particularly those in the South Boiler House, which have been in constant use for twenty years, are now in a very bad condition, and cannot be relied upon for service through another winter, and, notwithstanding the two new water tube boilers recently installed to replace some of these old boilers, there will not be sufficient steam-raising plant to meet next winter's load. It will, therefore, be necessary either to extend the boiler plant, or, alternatively, to arrange for an augmented supply of electrical energy from some other source."

3 One of the steam engine and dynamo sets that supplied power to Hampstead, pictured inside the Dynamo Room, 1899 (apparently maintained with a single small oilcan!).

2 Assistant Engineers Leadbeater (left) and Sayer (right) pictured inside the Switch-house at the Central Supply Station, Lithos Road, Hampstead, in 1899. [LEB Archive]

"Knowing the extreme difficulties encountered in obtaining the necessary sanction for our last two extensions, and having regard to the recent Electricity Supply Act and our lack of water for condensing purposes, I am of the opinion that no further extension of this generating station would be sanctioned by the Electricity Commissioners, to whom all such questions and schemes must now be submitted for approval. In accordance, therefore, with the Lighting Committee's instructions, I have been in negotiation with the two nearest outside sources for such a supply, *viz.*, the London & North-Western Railway Co. and the Borough of St Marylebone Electricity Supply."

Subsequently, "We have since been informed by the Electricity Commissioners that the London & North-Western Railway Co. have no power [*i.e.* authority] to supply; it is therefore unnecessary to go in detail into their proposal." [The Metropolitan Railway had also been approached, and rejected for the same reason.]

"The St Marylebone supply is 3-phase current at 50 periods [cycles] per second, which is to be the standard periodicity, at 6,600 volts. Their generating station is in Richmond Street, St John's Wood[3], a distance of approximately 2¼ miles from our generating station, about half of which is in the St Marylebone area and half in Hampstead. The St Marylebone Council have conduits with spare ducts already laid to within about 265 yards of the boundary in Abbey Road (Boundary Road), and they would be prepared to lay the necessary cables up to the boundary free of cost. We have conduits with spare ducts already laid from the power station down West End Lane to the top of Quex Road, so that to connect up with St Marylebone at the Borough boundary it would only be necessary to lay conduits from West End Lane along Abbey Road, a distance of approximately 750 yards. To do this, and to provide and lay cables in the existing conduits the whole distance from Boundary Road to the power station, would cost approximately £8,744."

Demotion to substation

The bulk supply of electricity from St Marylebone commenced in April 1921 and the Central Supply Station at Lithos Road ceased to generate from 25 August 1922, ten weeks ahead of planned closedown. At that date the undertaking had 24,675 consumers and a maximum load of 19,890 kW. St Marylebone's 6,600-volt, three-phase supply was converted at Lithos Road to two-phase (using Scott-connected transformers, and distributed at 2,000 volts single-phase with balanced feeders. Hampstead had generated at 90 cycles per second, but the new supply from St Marylebone was at 50 cycles per second, so every meter had to be changed and consumers' motors either changed or re-wound.

After a series of high-voltage faults in 1929 during which the whole of Hampstead was blacked out, the Metropolitan Borough of Hampstead engaged Sparks and Partners to report into the causes of the breakdowns. The consultants reported that "When Lithos Road was a generating station it had technically trained engineers on the premises night and day, but when it became a main sub-station it was staffed by sub-station attendants without technical supervision during long periods of the year. Technical control is necessary to minimise delay in renewing supply when emergencies occur." The report went on to say: "A Senior Technical Assistant, as well as a Senior Jointer, should either live at Lithos Road or in premises immediately adjoining the same." Soon after this report was published a garage with four flats over was built in the yard on the site of the old disinfecting station.

In 1932 the main office block comprised:

Ground floor Showroom and Cashier for payment of accounts.

First floor Offices of the Electrical Engineer and Manager and his Deputy; Public Lighting Office and Drawing Office; Correspondence Office for typing and despatch; Meter Fixers' Office and General

4 Electricity workers' annual outing, 1906. Behind the horses are the original offices which survived until 1974, on the left the main station chimney. Immediately behind the charabanc is the coal delivery siding, in the background the South Boiler House chimney dating from 1900/1. [LEB Archive]

Engineering Mains Office.

Second floor Offices of Chief Accountant and Accounts Chief Clerk; General Accounts Office (Costing and Billing).

In 1935 two additional floors were built over the Stores. The first floor was taken by the Engineering Mains department and the second floor by the Accounts department.

The Electricity Supply (Meters) Act 1936 required certain standards for meter testing and in 1939 two additional floors were added over the main sub-station for use by the Meter Superintendent for meter testing.

Nationalisation

At Vesting Day, 1 April 1948, Hampstead had 30,800 consumers and 269.5 miles of cables laid. The area of the Lithos Road site owned by the newly formed London Electricity Board (LEB) was 8,689 square yards and it rented a further 1,638 square yards from British Railways at £25 pa. The engineers and staff used three cars and there were five lorries and vans taken over from the late Borough of Hampstead Electric Supply Department.

The Cottage was still being lived in and was let to an employee for 12s 6d a week. The four flats over the garages were still in use and were also let to LEB employees at £1 a week. The Lithos Road offices formed the centre for Hampstead District of the North Western Sub-Area. The Accounts Department was moved from Lithos Road to Aybrook Street, St Marylebone, and its space was taken over by the Sub-Area Meter and Test Department.

Reorganisation

This arrangement continued until 1955, when the Meter and Test Department moved to Fulham and West Ham. Lithos Road then became the offices for the newly formed North Western District, which brought together the formerly separate Hampstead and Willesden districts.

In December 1958 a new showroom opened in Finchley Road and the old showroom in the area under the Manager's office at Lithos Road was put to other uses – a meter fixers' department and a security office.

In 1964 part of the old Central Supply Station was knocked down and the new Lithos Road 'A' Main Sub-Station was built by Higgs and Hill, while Jaggers built the new Lithos Road 'B' Main Sub-Station in 1966 – the same year that Murphys laid new 66,000-volt transmission cables into Lithos Road 'A' Sub-Station. (The 'B' Sub-Station has never been equipped.)

Another reorganisation took place on 1 November 1970 and the new *Regency* District of LEB was formed, which included all of the London Borough of Camden, half the Borough of Brent (Willesden) and a tiny corner of Ealing known as 'Greenford Detached'.

As the existing district offices at Lithos Road could not hold all the staff, some employees were accommodated at Triton Square (Euston Road), Short's Gardens (Covent Garden) and Aybrook Street. About 60 clerical staff of the newly formed Customer Services department were housed in temporary accommodation in Lithos Road yard.

New offices built

In October 1970 the LEB Head Office approved the provision of new District Offices and an Industrial Staff Depot at Lithos Road, which involved the demolition of all existing office buildings. The scheme provided accommodation for up to 250 office staff, who were housed on two floors of open-plan office space above the existing 'A' and 'B' Main Sub-Stations. The offices were designed on the principle of integrated environmental design and were linked by a two-storey bridge to the three-storey industrial block. The scheme allowed for 415 industrial staff housed on two floors above the new stores, together with the canteen and social facilities above. Also included in the scheme were workshops for transport maintenance and electrical fitting staff. The cost of the whole scheme was an estimated £805,000 and it was completed in 1974/5.

New offices demolished

The new offices and depot at Lithos Road were very short-lived. On 1 November 1983, a new LEB depot opened at City Road, Islington, covering the whole of the former Lithos Road area, plus Islington, Hackney and the City of London. The 'A' and 'B' Main Sub-Stations remain at Lithos Road, but the new offices were demolished and replaced with housing. Thus Lithos Road ended its 89-year history as the 'electric light office' for Hampstead (Fig 5).

Electricity supplied at present from Lithos Road is at the standard 11,000-volt three-phase, transformed down to 230/400 volts for domestic and light industrial use. Up on Hampstead Heath, however, there is an amazing survivor. A short section of the old Borough of Hampstead network (from Spaniards End to Dairy Cottage, Kenwood) is still running at 2,000 volts single-phase, 53 years after nationalisation, and 11 years after re-privatisation.

Notes and References

1 The London & Hampstead Battery Co Ltd had been supplying electric current since 1892 for the lighting of houses by means of overhead wires.
2 I remember my father (a high-tension cable jointer with the Borough of Hampstead Electric Supply) claiming that all Hampstead cats had striped bottoms because they insisted on sitting atop the pavement-level gridirons above the hot transformers. (PGS)
3 Richmond Street was later renamed Orchardson Street. A National Grid sub-station has now replaced the old St Marylebone Generating Station.

Sources

H M Land Registry Title Deeds.
Vestry of St John, Hampstead, *Introduction of the Electric Light, October 1st, 1894* (1894).
Vestry of St John, Hampstead, and Metropolitan Borough of Hampstead, *Minutes*, particularly those of the *Lighting Committee*.
Emile Garcke, *Manual of Electrical Undertakings* (various editions, 1898 onwards).
J M Knapman & F W Walker, "Hampstead to the Fore" in *London Electricity*, Nov/Dec 1958.
London Electricity Board, *Lithos House, Hampstead* (1975).

Brian Cox, Bob Gilham and **Peter Scott** were all employees of the London Electricity Board who worked in the Engineering Department at Lithos Road. Brian Cox and Bob Gilham originally wrote this article in the early 1970s.

Peter Scott has been a member of the Camden History Society since 1975, and in 1996 gained an MPhil degree in English Local History from the University of Leicester. He recently rescued the entire London Electricity Board Archive (over 1500 items) which had been languishing with the pigeons at Old Brompton Road Main Sub-Station. It is now at the London Metropolitan Archives, Clerkenwell.

5 A once familiar Hampstead address and telephone number – from a transformer chamber doorplate (actual size 5 x 12 in.).

The school for sons and orphans of missionaries
in Mornington Crescent, 1852-7

by David L Jones

On 26 November 1841 a group of ministers and a few layman from the London Missionary Society, the missionary branch of the Congregational churches, met in the Mission House at 4 Blomfield Street, Finsbury Circus and unanimously passed the following resolution:

That considering the extreme difficulty to which our missionary brethren are subject in obtaining a suitable education for their children in the countries where they reside, and the serious practical inconveniences connected with placing them at boarding schools in England, it appears to this meeting most desirable that an institution be formed for the accomplishment of that object.

In fact, the word *children* should have been *sons*, for a school for missionaries' daughters had been founded in Walthamstow four years earlier and the Society was simply trying to provide a similar institution for boys. The girls' school subsequently moved to Sevenoaks, where it is still known under its original title of "Walthamstow Hall".

A hundred and fifty years ago the formalities of starting up a school were less formidable than they are now. A house for the boys' school was rented in Walthamstow in what is now the High Street but was then known as Marsh Lane, and a headmaster was engaged. He was the Rev E Davies, who had served for five years as a missionary in Penang but been obliged by ill health to return to this country. On 1 January 1842 the school opened with nine boys and by October the number had increased to fourteen. The following year the Baptist Missionary Society joined the scheme.

Records of the first ten years are scant, but clearly the house was inadequate, and the Committee was already considering moving when the landlord forced their hand by terminating the lease in April 1847, refusing to grant them an additional 6 months while they stepped up the search for new premises. So for a while the boys were dispersed to various other schools in Peckham, Woolwich and even Windsor. By 1849 there were only 13 boys left, and they were sent to Dr Bell's School in Stockwell. These thirteen names are the earliest recorded in the school archives.

The move to Camden Town

General enthusiasm among the school's supporters, however, was at a low ebb. More than one committee meeting failed to obtain a quorum and they were selling off the school furniture to meet their debts. The faithful few, however, persisted, and in January 1852 the school reopened at what was then No.1 Mornington Crescent, which became No.36 in the renumbering that took place before the end of the century, on the corner of Arlington Street (now Arlington Road). As the school grew it became necessary to rent the adjoining house, No.2 (now No.35).

To relaunch the school the Committee luckily found exactly the headmaster they needed. W G Lemon was a man of determination yet kindness, and incredibly young for the position. Born in 1831, he celebrated his 21st birthday during his first year as Head. It is recorded that he seldom used the cane, yet was highly respected by the boys. When he relinquished the headship in 1866 he had seen the school re-established in even better accommodation (for those days) in Blackheath, and he became a barrister, being called to the Bar in 1866. He continued to serve the school, however, as Secretary to the Committee until the late 1880s, and died in 1897. He was also the first member of the London County Council to represent Lewisham. He had quite a remarkable family: one of his sons, Arthur Henry, became Governor of one of the Malayan colonies and another, Frank, became mayor of Reigate; Frank's wife was a founder of the RSPB.

One of Lemon's pupils at Mornington Crescent was Robert Moffat Livingstone, who attended the school from 1852 or earlier until 1856. A visitors' book in the school archives contains the signature of his father, David, spelt without the final **e.** Robert M Livingston(e) was killed in the American Civil War (school records are uncertain which side he was fighting on, or why).

A picture of the building at this time (Fig 1) indicates that the entrance to No.1 was actually in Arlington Street (now Road), but it is difficult to be clear on this point. Our main, indeed practically our only, source of information is a memoir written by a missionary, George B Stallworthy, who attended the school from 1855 to 1859, and in 1907 described to a meeting of Old Boys what life had been like in the old days 50 years before. He refers to an iron arch over the doorway, with a bracket for the link, but he does not say whether it actually faced into Mornington Crescent.

Memoirs of an Old Boy

Stallworthy describes life in the school quite minutely. He complains that even the staff of a school founded exclusively for missionaries' sons did not appreciate that to youngsters setting foot in England for the first time, life in London was as exotic as life in China, Samoa or Ceylon would have been to the teachers. The boys' first view of a steam train filled them with terror, and few of them could tell a daisy from a buttercup even though they might be well versed in the local flora of their earlier homes. They never visited Regent's Park or Kew Gardens. Since the school itself had no garden they used an old stable building in Arlington Street as a covered playground.

When Stallworthy left Samoa his mother was probably already dead, and the sight of his father being rowed back from the ship to the shore was the last time he would ever see him. A few days later the ship picked up two more boys bound for the same school; the elder one, who later became a judge in the High Court of Calcutta, did not see his father again for 33 years, and the younger one had died before this reunion took place. Such was the lot of the missionary families, yet they endured it all "for Christ's sake and the gospel's".

Some of the arrangements of the two houses can be gleaned from Stallworthy's memoirs. They were linked internally only on the ground floor; from the window of the schoolroom on the first floor the boys could see the yellow cabs passing along the Hampstead Road. There were dormitories on the upper floors and Stallworthy recalls that the more daring boys would move from one dormitory to another by climbing out of a window and walking along the narrow concrete ledge (see Fig 1) that ran along the outer wall of the building below the top floor windows. None of them ever had an accident. Washing facilities were downstairs; there was one bath which each boy used once a fortnight on Fridays – bathing in pairs with "the cook sponging hot water at one end and a housemaid at the other".

The curriculum was no doubt classical and, being designed for missionaries' sons, biblical. At breakfast the boys all had to recite the Ten Commandments in Latin (and at the top table in Greek), but it is perhaps a sign of Mr Lemon's slightly unorthodox – one can hardly say progressive – views that when the school migrated to Blackheath this custom was dropped in favour of reciting two verses from the Book of

16   Camden History Review   Vol.25 (2001)

Proverbs. German and French were both on the curriculum, the former taught by Herr Christian Mast, who later went to open a school of his own in Belgravia, and the latter by a series of Frenchmen whose poor grasp of English rendered them totally incapable of maintaining order or teaching their own language. Mr Lemon insisted, however, on a broader curriculum than simply the classics and languages. There were half-hour periods for reading Greek and Roman history, and each term he would hand out treatises on subjects such as astronomy and geology. There were no penalties for not indulging in the delights of these subjects, but there were prizes for boys who showed they had read the material attentively. It is not stated who paid for the prizes, but, since the school was running on a shoestring, it was probably Mr Lemon himself. The one subject that did not figure in the school's life was Chemistry.

That did not mean that chemical experiments were not tried. A boy called Thomson possessed a miniature brass cannon and he had somehow managed to acquire a small supply of gunpowder. Unfortunately, when he tried to operate the gun in the covered playground he held his face too close to it and had a narrow escape. A more deliberate escapade occurred around the same time when two boys, whose names are not disclosed, actually ran away. Three days later they were found wandering in the dock area and returned to Mornington Crescent, and the Rev Mr Harrison from Park Chapel was asked to come and address the whole school on the sins of ingratitude and insubordination.

One possible benefit may have come from this episode: it opened the eyes of the Committee to the inadequacy of the premises for their purpose, and their search for a new property gained some urgency. One of the leading lights in establishing the school at Mornington Crescent had been a Miss E J Peek (of the biscuit family), and again she busied herself in looking for a suitable site, eventually finding one near Blackheath Station, and thither the whole school moved in November 1857.

Sources

1 Clifford Witting (ed.) *Glory of the Sons, a history of Eltham College*, 1952, republished and updated as *Past and Present*, ed. C Porteous, 1992. Both published by Eltham College.
2 Reminiscences of George Stallworthy, 1907. Issued by Eltham College Archives, 2000 (copy deposited in Camden Archives Centre).
3 Family research by Mr T R Lemon.

David L Jones is the Archivist of Eltham College (formerly the School for the Sons of Missionaries).

1 Institution for the Sons of Missionaries at No.1 (now 36) Mornington Crescent, Hampstead Road, 1852–7.

A short history of Oak Village

by William Barnes

The history of Oak Village falls conveniently into three periods. The first covers about 20 years between 1850 and 1870, when the Gospel Oak area was being developed out of little more than nothing, in response to the rapidly growing population of north London. The second is a period of some 90 years, incorporating two world wars, when the people of Gospel Oak lived more or less placidly in the small, neat houses that had been built, watching them gradually deteriorate but without the means to prevent this. The third period began in 1962 when a vigorous Labour Council, in what was soon to be the London Borough of Camden, embarked on a policy of wholesale demolition followed by replacement with large blocks of flats, a policy fiercely resisted by the residents of Oak Village, Julia Street and Elaine Grove, so that these three streets survived in very much their mid-Victorian garb.

The Gospel Oak

We begin with the Gospel Oak. It is clearly shown on a map of 1801 standing very near the point where Malden Road now joins Southampton Road. There are various candidates for the distinction of having preached the Gospel under this oak tree and thus of giving it its name. The first is Saint Augustine of Canterbury, who in AD 597 brought Christianity to the south of England. There is no evidence that he ever came to this part of the country and, though oaks are known to survive for 1000 years or more, it is unlikely that a tree still standing at the beginning of the 19th century was also standing at the end of the 6th. A second candidate is the 14th-century philosopher, theologian and reformer John Wycliffe. The third and fourth candidates are John Wesley (1703–1791), who is credited with having begun the practice of field-preaching, and his close associate George Whitefield (1714–177), leader of the Calvinistic Methodists and founder in 1756 of the Chapel in the Tottenham Court Road. One of these last two perhaps deserves the credit.

A more likely reason for the name of Gospel Oak is that the tree stood very near the boundary with the parish of Hampstead. It was (and is) the custom to have an annual perambulation of the bounds, and the St Pancras Vestry minutes of 5 December 1821 set out in detail the route of such perambulations. The minute says at the end "Then proceed in the same southerly line and along the south side of the north hedge of the seven following fields, in the last of which is the Gospel Oak Field and near the path is a St Pancras stone where the oak formerly stood."(The parish map dated c.1804, Fig 1, shows a Hampstead Stone and a St Pancras stone standing next to each other in Gospel Oak Field.) A short sermon was preached to the assembled party during this 'beating of the bounds'; John Richardson has suggested[1] that the tree was the site for this sermon, giving it the name of Gospel Oak. It was reached at the end of an exhausting hike round the boundaries and was the logical place for a short religious service. It seems that one or more stones had replaced the tree by 1810: the Vestry minute quoted makes it clear that the tree was not there in 1821. Another St Pancras Vestry minute (13 April 1854) mentions a proposal to mark the site of the Gospel Oak by erecting a stone: perhaps this was to replace the earlier stone. Another Vestry decision in 1854 was to place a memorial plaque to the old oak near the Southampton Road railway bridge, but this decision was never given effect. There was, however, a pub in Southampton Road called The Gospel Oak.

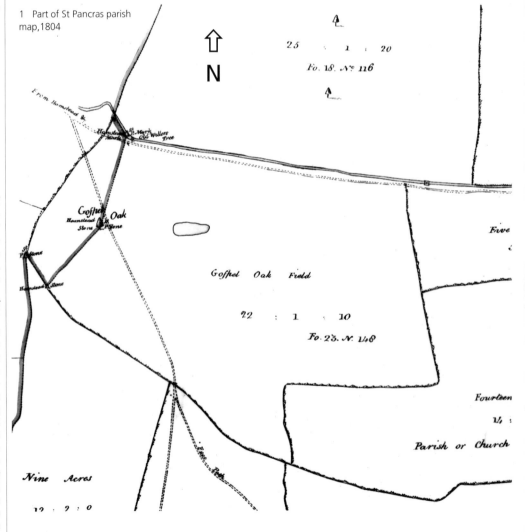

1 Part of St Pancras parish map, 1804

2 Miniature of (the 1st) Viscount Lismore, ? around 1810

What is certain is that by the time the railways came in the 19th century, the Gospel Oak had reached the end of its life and had disappeared. It is also certain that the Old Oak pub in Mansfield Road, opposite Gospel Oak Station, is not built on the site of the tree. In 1998 Michael Palin planted a new oak tree in the little-used community garden in Lismore Circus, and a plaque there commemorates this event.

Early history

Gospel Oak Field and the area immediately south of it originally belonged to the FitzRoy family. Their ancestor the Duke of Grafton (b.1662 of the liaison between Charles II and Barbara Villiers, created Duchess of Cleveland) had acquired extensive lands around Kentish Town, large parts of which had to be sold later to pay gambling debts. However, some remained in the FitzRoys' manor of Tottenhall until the 19th century. In 1806 Lord Ferdinand FitzRoy, the then lord of the manor, sold some land to Viscount Lismore (Fig 2), an Irish peer (1775–1857) who was until 1838 Lord Lieutenant of Tipperary. Colonel Charles FitzRoy, who was created Baron Southampton in 1780, held all the land to the west of this as far as Haverstock Hill (and to the south as far as what is now Fitzroy Square) until the major Southampton sale in 1840 and the purchase by the Orphan Working School in 1841 of a considerable estate adjacent to Haverstock Hill. Apart from the acres on which the school itself was built, this was later developed as Maitland Park. Soon afterwards Lord Lismore, then in his 70s, laid out the Circus that now bears his name and its feeder roads, and then auctioned the rest of his land in small lots to builders and developers. Fig 3 shows the plans, with the names of some of the small landowners, in 1845. Soon the Circus itself contained flower-beds, with a fence around them locked at night. But progress on building was slow.

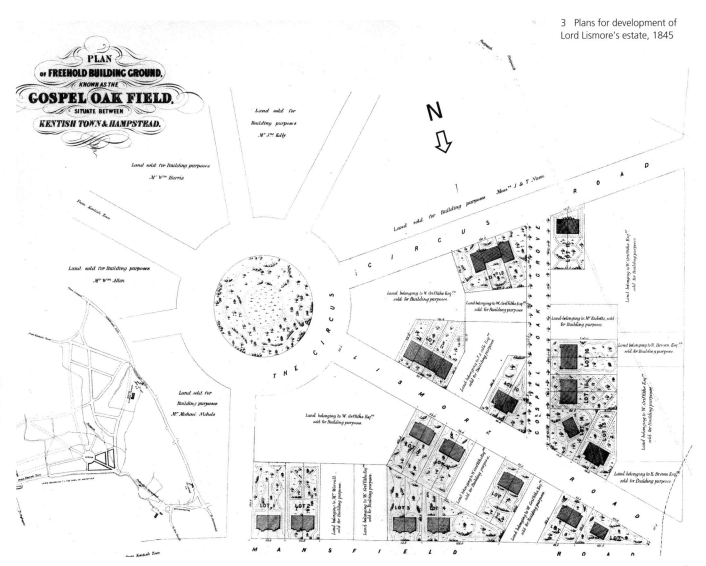

3 Plans for development of Lord Lismore's estate, 1845

Camden History Review Vol.25 (2001)

Lismore Circus, "island of mud"

Until 1850, Gospel Oak was a rather inaccessible spot, isolated from both Hampstead and Kentish Town and distant from main roads. The various small landlords were unable to get together and agree on a project to lay it out handsomely. Ten years later no-one had yet bothered to build a proper carriageway from Highgate Road, and the remoteness of Gospel Oak, instead of being rural, was becoming squalid. In 1867 Lismore Circus, planned years before, was still a "mud island". A letter to the local paper complains of "the dank, pot-holed state of the road-way lying at the back of Oak Village. Vehicles can only approach our dwellings by a long and roundabout detour. We are completely isolated from the civilised world." Even in 1851, there were no buildings on the brave street pattern (Fig 3) centred on the Circus. By 1853 there were still only "some 12 or 13 houses, with a beer shop at the corner", apparently "the favourite resort of navvies and quarrelsome shoemakers" (ref.2, p 164).

In 1855 a couple called Karl and Jenny Marx, later to achieve world-wide fame, moved from what Jenny described as the 'old hole' in Soho to 9 Grafton Terrace, just across Malden Road, and not far from the site of the old Gospel Oak tree. This house was classified as third class by the Metropolitan Building Office and was let at an annual rent of £36, which was regarded as cheap for North London. The rent was mostly paid by their friend, Friedrich Engels: Marx was totally hopeless with money and usually in debt. Jenny Marx wrote[3] *"Our attractive little house, though it was like a palace for us in comparison with the places we have lived before, was not easy to get to. There was no smooth road leading to it, building was going on all around, one had to pick one's way over heaps of rubbish and, in rainy weather, the sticky red soil caked to one's boots so that it was a tiring struggle and with heavy feet that one reached our house. And then it was dark in those wild districts, so that, rather than have to tackle the dark, the rubbish, the clay and the heaps of stones, one preferred to spend the evenings by a warm fire. I was very unwell that winter and was always surrounded with stacks of medicine bottles."* A few years later they moved further west to what is now the Maitland Park Estate, the area around the Orphan Working School, mentioned earlier.

Progress by 1860

A map of 1860 (Fig 4) shows nine houses built along Circus Road, west of the Circus. A new (short-lived) road, Lismore Road, also led out of the Circus, joining Mansfield Road at the corner of Southampton Road (where the traffic lights are now), with a group of 12 small houses at that corner. Strangely, when all this land was laid out, Lismore Circus itself was not conveyed to anybody. The Vestry was still arguing about this in the 1890s. In 1890 it was opened to the public: then, because of complaints about the noise of children, shut again; then reopened in 1899. Beyond the corner of Lismore and Mansfield Roads, the map shows a 'footway to Hampstead', presumably along the line of the Fleet river, now Fleet Road; and a little to the east of the corner was a short road called Gospel Oak Grove, with five little houses joining Lismore Road to Circus Road.

Oak Village itself had been partially built up by 1860 (Fig 4). For the uninitiated, one must explain that the name *Oak Village* is applied to houses built on two parallel roads leading south from Mansfield Road *plus* a double-sided street ("Long Oak Village") projecting west from the western 'strip' (see the bottom left-hand group of houses in 4, across Mansfield

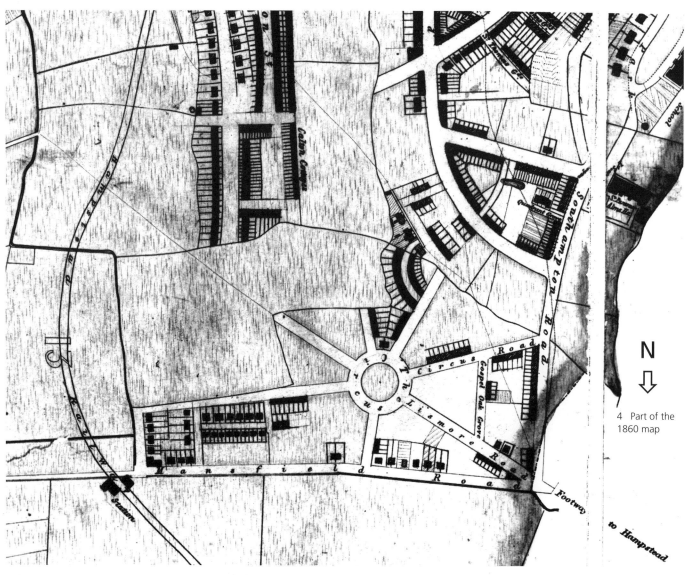

4 Part of the 1860 map

Road from the railway station).

There were 13 semi-detached houses in the 'strips' of Oak Village leading south from Mansfield Road, with a further six or seven actually in Mansfield Road, where the shops next to the Old Oak pub now are. To the west of Long Oak Village there was a group of three houses at the corner of what is now Julia Street; Elaine Grove did not yet exist, except for two semi-detached houses up towards the Circus.

Eight years later, in 1868 (Fig 5), Oak Village itself was little changed, but Arthur Grove (later to change its name to Elaine Grove) had been created, with about 20 houses on either side. There were also a dozen houses on the north side of the Circus itself, and another dozen along the eastern stretch of Circus Road (now Lamble Street, named in 1887 after a popular member of the Vestry).

In the 1860s the whole Gospel Oak area, including Oak Village, was actively developed as a series of small streets with mostly small houses. The names of the streets changed with bewildering frequency. The 1880s saw a similar development on the other side of Mansfield Road, with rather taller houses. For the next 80 years, despite two world wars with bombs falling on the district, it had a comparatively quiet time. (Happy the country which has no history.)

Coming of the railways

This district, being near the manor of Hampstead to the west and Lord Mansfield's Kenwood estate to the north, should in theory have been well favoured for residential development, but it was blighted before it came into being by the coming of the railways in the middle of the 19th century. Already by 1850, the Hampstead Railway had been built along the southern boundary of Hampstead Heath, to the north of Mansfield Road. This line (now the North London Line), which first headed for Camden Town and then struck eastwards, curved south soon after passing the area under consideration, somewhat to the east of our district. More devastating still, in the early 1860s came the Midland Railway, on its way from Finchley Road to St Pancras via Kentish Town. It passed through tunnels under the parish of Hampstead before surfacing at Lismore Circus, where there was a station, slicing off one side of Vicar Street (now Vicar's Road) as it did so (Fig 5), and then passed straight along one of Lismore's spokes to the Kentish Town station. In planning the route William Tite, the architect retained by the Midland, in evidence at an enquiry in 1853 characteristically described the few properties existing at Gospel Oak (which of course had to be demolished) as 'humble', adding "I do not mean to say they are to be disregarded because they are humble, but some of them are very inferior, very ill-built and wretched" (ref.2, p 165). Finally, in 1868 the Tottenham and Hampstead Junction Railway came in from the east, locally from Holloway Road, to join the Hampstead Line very near Gospel Oak station.

The result of all this was that a large area between Highgate Road and Grafton Road lay beneath interconnecting railway lines (see Fig 5) and their associated buildings and yards. Much smoke and noise now emanated from this rectangle of former farm land, and this led to a drastic reduction of the social status of West Kentish Town as well as the building of factories on the west side of Highgate Road.

The Midland's terminus at St Pancras was built in 1868, and a letter in the press that year complained (ref.2, p 167) that the dispossessed poor of Agar Town, over the flattened remains of which the approach

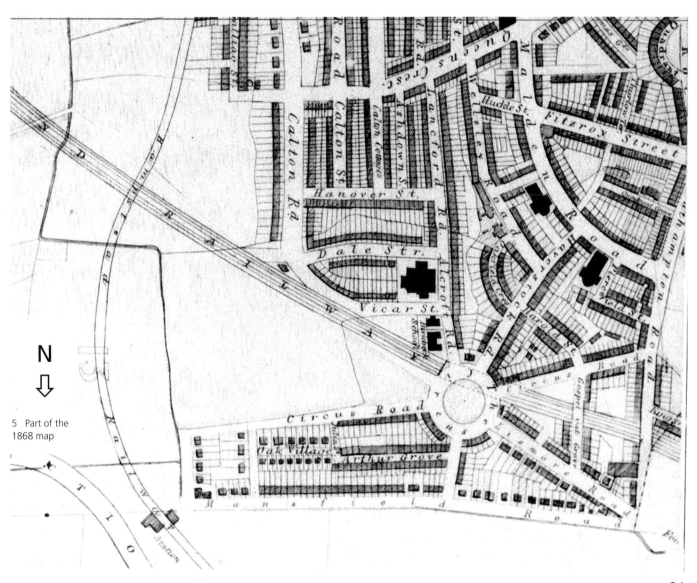

5 Part of the 1868 map

to the station had been built, were now "crowding and lowering in character the once promising locality springing up, known as the Oak Village". (The name of Oak Village seems to date from this time.) To make their line possible, the Midland needed to build two tunnels, the first in 1866 and the second in 1883. The company was very astute: while the Bill authorising them to build their new line was going through Parliament, they steadily bought up the land around the proposed line, and the buildings on it, mainly from St Pancras Church Lands. When the Act was passed, they were ready to proceed. They suppressed the traditional Gospel Oak Easter Fair. They pulled down all the houses behind the Mitre pub in Grafton Road, but left the pub itself to slake the thirsts of the railway workers. A light railway was built to carry spoil and bricks from behind the Mitre as far as Southampton Road. The tract of land south-east of Oak Village became a spoil heap and, despite an attempt to sell the spoil to those building the Thames Embankment, it so remained for the best part of 100 years, when Kiln Place was built (1950s), on the site of a brick-works.

Horses, trams and churches

What of the environs, and services for the new district? Even though in 1867 Lismore Circus was still "a mud island, completely isolated from the civilised world" (ref.2, p 167), John Derby Allcroft, MP of Stokesay Court, Shropshire, and owner of the prosperous firm Dent's Gloves, had two years earlier been persuaded to part with £35,000 in memory of his wife "to provide a church for a needy and populous area". This built St Martin's Church and endowed the parish. The church stands just across the Midland's mainline railway from Oak Village. It was designed by the architect E B Lamb and built, together with the vicarage opposite, in 1865. The tower at St Martin's was, and is, 130 feet high and when it was built it was said to stand higher than any tower in London. In those days it had a 'spirelet' which added to its height. A century later Allcroft's granddaughter Lady Allcroft-Magnus, wife of Sir Philip Magnus, the historian and biographer of Gladstone,

was still patron, though she lived far away in Shropshire. Nikolaus Pevsner described St Martin's as "the craziest of London's Victorian churches". It celebrated its centenary in 1965, when considerable renovations were carried out.

The 1868 map (Fig 5) shows Birkbeck School just to the north of the church and vicarage, on the site where the Council offices and Scout Hall are now. Birkbeck School derived its name from George Birkbeck (1776–1841), pioneer of accessible lectures on science for working men in Glasgow, who went on to found the Mechanics Institution in London in 1824 and helped found University College, London in 1827. But this school was founded by William Ellis, who founded ten schools with the aim of including the teaching of political economy in elementary education, naming them in honour of George Birkbeck. Ellis (1800–1881), of Huguenot origin, established the Gospel Oak Schools in 1862 in Rochford Street, off Lismore Circus. Ellis wanted pupils not to learn by rote, but to think for themselves. In 1864, however, the Rochford Street site was bought by the Midland Railway and the school had to move a short distance away to Allcroft Road (off Queen's Crescent) with nearly 800 pupils. Over the years nine of William Ellis's ten schools have disappeared: the tenth moved in 1937 to Highgate Road, where it is still is.

Interestingly, two further churches are shown in Fig 5 on Malden Road, one where there is now a garage and the other now occupied by Simpson's Bicycle Shop. One of these was St Andrew's, designed by Charles Hayward and opened in 1866.

The 1860 and the 1868 maps both show the 'footway to Hampstead' along what is now Fleet Road. The first houses in Fleet Road were built soon after 1860 and the Methodist Church was constructed there in 1865, the same year that saw the building of St Martin's.

In 1880 three things happened. Horse-drawn trams travelling from London up Southampton Road were introduced (they were electrified in 1909 and continued to run until 1938); South End Green came into existence with its fountain designed by Samuel Teulon; and Fleet Road School was started and became known as the "Harrow of Board Schools".

Lord Mansfield deplored the coming of the trams, and in this he was supported by Sir Rowland Hill (1795–1873), who occupied a large estate where Rowland Hill Street now runs eastwards from Haverstock Hill. Just below his house, where the Royal Free now stands, was a fever hospital, admitting smallpox patients. Neither Mansfield nor Hill was keen on the inferior beings who caught smallpox and/or travelled by tram, and did not want them spreading into Hampstead. Mansfield therefore built a wall on the Hampstead/St Pancras boundary, where Savernake Road becomes Constantine Road near the present bridge to the Heath, in an attempt to prevent any further houses built to the west of this wall being other than of a good middle-class standard. Other locals, however, appointed the Rev Charles Mackeson, the popular local preacher, as their spokesman to protest against these high-handed actions. In 1891 Lord Mansfield finally agreed to pull the wall down and in 1895 the bridge over the railway to Hampstead Heath was constructed. In 1892 the foundation stone of All Hallows, to be built on land purchased from Lord Mansfield, was laid, but Mackeson did not live to see its inauguration (1901).

From 1914 to 1945

A bomb falling in Allcroft Road in WW I is alleged to have been the first to fall in Britain: the bodies were carried away in horse-drawn dust carts. In WW II, the large brick-built school in Mansfield Road, near the railway station, was bombed, together with several houses opposite: it was rebuilt in the 1960s as Gospel Oak School. Tom Dixon (vicar of St Martin's 1967–77) relates[4] that residents of Gospel Oak frequently used to climb up Parliament Hill to see whether after a night of bombing the City of London was still there.

Outside the two wars, life in Oak Village was comparatively calm. The area was well supplied with public houses: there was an inn (known as the Mansfield Hotel), perhaps built for the tramway age, on the corner of Mansfield Road and Southampton Road, with public conveniences beside it; there was a large pub known as the Duke of Cornwall on the corner of Elaine Grove facing Lismore

Circus; and there was another pub called the Wheatsheaf not far away. Almost opposite the Duke of Cornwall a street called Heriot Place led from Lismore Circus to the shops in Mansfield Road. 'Old inhabitant' Rose Clutton, speaking in 1999 about her childhood in Elaine Grove during and after WW I, could remember the names of many shops in and around Lismore Circus: Rackham's the greengrocers, and Leach's provision shop in Heriot Place, Taverner's furniture shop, Hall's the builders, Phillips another vegetable shop, Austin's provision shop and, on the other side of Lismore Road, a pawnshop, an off-licence and a dairy. She was also told of a stream near Lismore Road with a bungalow over it in which people used to fish. Rochford Road used to run from 'a clinic' to Southampton Road and in it were a peasepudding shop, a shop with antiques and clothes, and yet another pub, the King Alfred, always called 'The Wreck'. Old Mr Mundy, who used to live in the village, also told her that there were no fewer than seven wells hereabouts.

The 1960s fight for preservation

In 1962 sweeping redevelopment plans for the area north of Queen's Crescent (Grafton and Gospel Oak wards) were set in motion, and started to take their relentless course. Over the next 14 years, much of the area was reduced to a wasteland of one kind or another – empty boarded houses; churned earth; blocks christened by the local people 'Colditz'. The exception was in Oak Village, which some[2] characterised as an enclave of battling, wealthy owner-occupiers. More accurately, perhaps, a mixed group of owner-occupiers were determined to defend their homes.

In June 1966, David McKie wrote an article in the Express and News (now more familiar as the Ham & High) saying that Camden Borough Council proposed to demolish Oak Village as part of the redevelopment scheme, but that people living in Oak Village were planning to set up a housing co-operative in the hope of saving their houses. He described the village as two small streets of Victorian houses built in a simple but sturdy style which, despised or neglected for many years, was then coming back into fashion in several parts of London. He said that the records showed that these houses were not, as some believed, built for the workers at the nearby brickworks, but for the middle classes. Recently a London company, Edwards Estates Ltd, had bought up eighteen of them, refurbishing and reselling eight or nine of them at £11,000 each. Others had been bought privately and, following more extensive refurbishing, were worth as much as £15,000. Almost unbelievably, Camden Council had been giving improvement grants on some of these as late as 1965. The Director of Planning at the time was a colourful and powerful character called Dr Bruno Schlaffenberg. He did not want to retain terraces, such as those in Oak Village, which had been designed to stand for only 60 years. Peggy Duff, Chairman of the Planning Committee, was much influenced by Schlaffenberg.

The residents of Oak Village were in fact split as regards future policy. The middle-class 'newcomers' were joined by some of the working-class people who had lived there all their lives in a protest movement to try and persuade the Council to exclude Oak Village and Elaine Grove from their redevelopment plans. Others in the village, who could not afford to modernise their homes, were eager to see the houses swept away so that they would be re-housed by the Council. Eventually Peggy Duff agreed, apparently reluctantly, to see if it was possible "to leave some of the better houses without doing great damage to the amenities of the whole scheme".

In 1968 an Environmental Survey was undertaken by the Camden Society of Architects, and a report on the Gospel Oak Area was prepared by Christopher Gotch. This records that the redevelopment of Gospel Oak began soon after WW II with the building of the multi-storeyed 'slab' Barrington Court, designed by the distinguished firm Powell and Moya, soon followed by the development of Lamble Street and Kiln Place. Christopher Gotch's report said that the area around Mansfield Road, once an area of modest neat little streets, had over a century and in recent years become totally unliveable through decay and lack of proper maintenance ('recent years' had of course included the war). The report went on to say that Oak Village and Elaine Grove were originally part of the over-

all 1960s plan but, due to the lapse of time in co-ordinating various parts of the large comprehensive development scheme, most of the houses in the two streets had been refurbished and sold to a wealthier and more vociferous section of the community. Gotch concluded that the houses possessed undeniable charm but that it remained to be seen if the decision to exclude them from the redevelopment would prove to be valid, or whether Oak Village and Elaine Grove would become an anachronism in the new neighbourhood.

The Bishop of Willesden, Graham Leonard, in appointing Tom Dixon as vicar of St Martin's in 1967, expressed the hope that he would help to rebuild a community in Gospel Oak. It was left to Dixon in the early 1970s to arrange for the demolition of the old vicarage and the building of a new one, with eight maisonettes and flats next door managed by the World of Property Housing Trust. A year or two later, the church tower and its derelict clock were repaired, the clock with a royal blue face and gold-leafed figures. The miniature spire was taken down. At the end of his time, Tom Dixon wrote a short book about his stewardship entitled *Operation Skyscraper*[4] which, despite his rather misleading title, is his claim to have done what the Bishop had asked him to do.

In February 1970 Camden Council announced that demolition at Gospel Oak was to go ahead and that "under the present housing programme, everyone will be leaving the older buildings that remain in the Gospel Oak redevelopment area during 1970 and 1971." Building was expected to start in April 1970 north of the main railway line and probably about a year later in the rest of the redevelopment area. This was described as bounded to the east by Grafton Road, railway land and Oak Village; to the north by Mansfield Road; and to the west and south by Southampton Road, Malden Road and Queen's Crescent. These boundaries did not prevent Heriot Place and the first eight houses in Elaine Grove, with the Duke of Cornwall pub opposite them, being swept away.

By 1971, the St Pancras Civic Society, in the persons of Diana Gurney, Jennie Marriott and Tammo de Jongh, had taken up the cudgels – but too

late. Writing in the *North London Press* (the old *Camden Journal*), they lamented that "what has happened to poor Gospel Oak is too awful for words". They admitted that the old Gospel Oak was in need of rehabilitation, but added "what a lovely, friendly place it could have been". They referred romantically to Lismore Circus with "charming little personal shops, a true centre for a community, with a garden full of pigeons, tall trees and a few seats where the old people spent the time of day." There is no specific reference to Elaine Grove or Oak Village in this article, but a claim that many ordinary working people had saved up enough money to put a deposit on a house. The authors added that such people could no longer afford the large sums demanded for those houses that were left and had to go to Stoke Newington or Hackney to find the character which in Camden had been destroyed.

By April 1972 Christopher Gotch, writing in the *Ham & High*, seems to have changed sides and decided to join the angels. "I ask you," he wrote, "is it not a blessing that Oak Village and Elaine Grove were saved from redevelopment? Only by dint of effort by those who cared were they saved. And now they remain as silent accusers to point the difference between the old and the new, the past and the present". Gotch's argument now takes a new line. The presence of preserved houses in Oak Village and Elaine Grove contrasts with the loss of Lismore Circus, but the houses themselves do not possess much intrinsic merit. They were merely a product of speculative building of their own period. His argument as an architect appears to be that the rescued houses in Oak Village are not architecture and what has replaced them in the rest of Gospel Oak is not architecture either. To provide enough housing in such a district of London, 'architecture' has to be sacrificed.

I take the opportunity, in concluding, to put the record straight about the attitudes of Camden Council in 1971 and the radical change soon thereafter. It is true that a pamphlet published in 1971 states that "the proportion of privately rented flats must be expected to fall and, with a vigorous housing programme, the number of Council dwellings must be expected to increase." But part-

ly because in the early 1970s the Architect's Department at Camden was overwhelmed by the number of Council estates it was building, and partly because of changes in the law, policy changed sharply in 1974. The aim now became to preserve and rehabilitate as many small houses as possible. No doubt the struggle put up by the inhabitants of Oak Village contributed to this. In 2000, a Government grant enabled Lismore Circus to be laid out once again, though at the time of writing – late 2000 – it is, as a consequence, once again an island in a sea of mud!

Acknowledgements

I owe a great deal to Michael Ogden RIBA, to John Richardson, Chairman of the Camden History Society, and to Miss Rose Clutton, who has lived at 9 Elaine Grove from an infant and is thus the 'oldest inhabitant' of Oak Village, for details. Any errors remain my own.

Sources

Camden History Society's *Kentish Town Packet* 1979
Debrett's *Peerage*
Dictionary of National Biography 1961
Christopher Gotch, Report on the Gospel Oak Area for Camden Council's Environmental Survey of 1968.
Maps, courtesy of Camden Local Studies and Archives Centre

References

1 Richardson, John *Kentish Town Past* Historical Publications Ltd 1997.
2 Tindall, Gillian *The Fields Beneath* Temple Smith 1977.
3 Wheen, Francis *Karl Marx* Fourth Estate 1999.
4 Dixon, Tom *Operation Skyscraper* Churchman 1988.

William Barnes moved to Oak Village in 1998. A resident of the Borough of Camden since before it was created, he acted as its Director of Housing in the 1970s. His home has been in the Mansfield Road Conservation Area for 20 years.

The Irish in Kilburn
and the Church of the Sacred Heart, Quex Road

by Michael Alpert

Immigration

The early and middle parts of the 19th century saw copious Irish immigration into England, Wales and Scotland. The Irish population of London has been estimated as having reached 50,000 by 1814.[1] Irish immigration increased markedly as a result of the famines of the 1840s, and this is reflected in numbers of Irish-born in the censuses of 1841, 1851 and 1861. However, in the censuses of 1871 and 1881 (and indeed through to 1901) the numbers were smaller, because the Irish communities – still characterised as such by their English neighbours – were now composed more of second-generation people not born in Ireland.[2] What may be called 'the 'Irish community' was thus larger than the censuses might indicate. There is also some doubt over whether the enumerators recorded all the transient and rough-living people in an area, many of whom may have been Irish.

Where the Irish lived

As central parts of London were steadily cleared of slums and rebuilt, the evicted population, some of it Irish, moved out. Quite early in the 19th century, there were Irish settlements in the Lisson Grove area of Paddington, bordering on Kilburn. Similar settlements may have arisen in connection with the construction, in the 1830s, of the London and Birmingham railway, which passed through Kilburn, and the associated extensive building work in that district. The census of 1851 already shows multiple occupation by Irish-born people of several houses in Kilburn Lane on the boundary of Kilburn.

1 Father Robert Cooke (from *Centenary Brochure of Oblate Fathers in Kilburn 1865–1965*)

Kilburn

Kilburn[3] was a district mostly in the Vestry of Willesden, but lying on both sides of the Edgware Road and bordering on the Metropolitan boroughs of Paddington and Hampstead. It stretched from Maida Vale in the south to Cricklewood in the north, eastwards as far as West End Lane and the area later called West Hampstead[4], and west of the Edgware Road along the Ranelagh river (later Kilburn Park Road), Carlton Road (later Carlton Vale) and Salusbury Road.

Religion

The major characteristic of the Irish, apart from their poverty, was their Catholic religion. As one author comments, *"The his-*

tory of the migration of the Irish to England is intimately bound up with the history of the spread and re-establishment of Catholicism in the last two centuries".[5]

In 1840, before the great migrations to England, there were only 26 Roman Catholic Churches in London. This was insufficient even for the English Catholics and may explain the neglect of religious duties noticed by observers. Cardinals Wiseman and Manning, the nineteenth century leaders of the Catholic Church in England, developed missions to serve the growing Catholic population, largely composed of poor and newly-arrived Irish. A historian of the Irish settlement in 19th century England writes: *"The number of priests increased, and the active role of the Church in organising its congregations grew enormously. Priests organised festivals, musical evenings, church suppers, excursions..."*.[6]

By 1850, the number of Catholic churches had risen to 104, served by 168 priests, 4 religious houses for men, 17 convents and a number of schools. The total Catholic population of England, Wales and Scotland rose from 600,000 in 1841 to 900,000 in 1861. Most of the increase consisted, in all likelihood, of Irish arrivals. Whether many of them came to Kilburn – later the quintessentially Irish district of London – is, however, uncertain.

The Oblates arrive

The present massive Catholic Church of the Sacred Heart, in Quex Road, in the middle of Kilburn, was founded by the Oblates of Mary Immaculate. The Oblates helped to remedy the general shortage in England of Irish-born clergy who could hear confessions in the native Gaelic of many of the immigrants. There seems, however, to be no connection between Irish settlement and the decision of Father Robert Cooke, Provincial Superior of the Oblates (Fig 1), to found this mission in Kilburn. When Fr. Cooke was at a retreat in July 1864, the Superior General of the Oblates, Fr. Fabre, asked him to approach Cardinal Wiseman to seek permission to allow missions to be opened in London.[7] Fr. Cooke later wrote that in 1865, in the public room of a London hotel, he overhead somebody saying: *"I have heard my brother, who is a priest of great experience, say that there was no suburb in London where a new mission and church were required more than in Kilburn"*.[8]

Fr. Cooke refers[9] mysteriously to special opportunities for a new mission in the suburbs of London, which would not present themselves later on. He may have meant the chance to buy the land in Quex Road. Soon, Fr. Cooke travelled to Kilburn, noting as he got off the omnibus at the Cock Tavern, nearly opposite Quex Road, *"All around were extensive fields, trees, wild flowers and a few scattered houses."* [10] The parish of Kilburn must have contrasted strongly with the dank slums of Tower Hill, in which the Oblates had been ministering to Irish immigrants.

One sultry evening in the summer of 1866, the Superior General of the Oblates and Father Cooke walked from Greville Road to the site of the new church in Quex Road. The ground was higher than the surroundings and one could survey most of Kilburn from it. Father Cooke wrote *"From all sides only wealthy houses can be seen. It is an aristocratic district, the healthiest in London and its surroundings. There is immense good to be done there. Before we arrived, Our Lord had no place of shelter there...Let us hope that our Fathers can establish a House in Kilburn which will become the centre of the English Province and a place of rest and relaxation for our Fathers in Tower Hill"*. [11]

Another Catholic body, the Passionist Fathers, who settled in Poplar House in what is now Inglewood Road in neighbouring West Hampstead, had come in 1848 to set up missions and in particular to help poor Irish immigrants. [12] This suggests that there may have been a population, perhaps unnoticed by the censuses, of transient and rough-living Irish in the area (though neither the local press nor local government documents provide any indication of this). It also seems that Fr. Cooke, whose mission succeeded, unlike that of the Passionists who had to move away to rural Kingsbury, [13] was looking for a rest-home for overworked clergy who were serving the Oblates' mission in London's dockland. As he wrote to the Superior General:

"Kilburn may be called a suburb of the city of London. On one side it adjoins the city proper, and on the other side it stretches out into the country. The air around Kilburn is reputed to be the purest and the least contaminated of all in London. We are fortunate enough to have become the owners of some land in this area. As soon as our resources permit, we shall build a church and a community residence in Kilburn. When this desired result is accomplished, our Fathers from Tower Hill will have an ideal place to retire from their laborious ministry and for a few days enjoy the consolation of quiet religious meditation and study". [14]

There was another consideration, however. Fr. Cooke and the Catholic journal *The Tablet* laid particular emphasis on the fact that the New Priory, as the residence of the Oblate Fathers was and is still called, was the successor, after 400 years, of the old Kilburn Priory, suppressed by Henry VIII. [15]

Mrs Malone

The Oblates rented No.1, Greville Road, a turning off Kilburn High Road, on 1 February 1865. The following day they celebrated Mass with five worshippers. In August 1866 they acquired 4 acres of the Connon estate in Quex Road for £4,000. Building began in 1867. On 8 September, the first Mass in the new church was celebrated. At this date there were still only 40 or 50 Catholics in Kilburn. [16] One wonders therefore whether the Oblates were trying to proselytise among the general population or if they were seeking to bring the benefits of religion to Irish Catholics such as those mentioned as living in Kensal New Town's 'Soapsuds Island', named for its proximity to local laundries in an area bounded by the canal, the railway and the gasworks. [17] The first mention in the local press to these Irish people appears in reference to a strike of washerwomen in Kensal New Town, superciliously reported in 1873 by the local newspaper, which referred to 'the contumacious Mrs. Maloney', though indeed paying some awed respect to the very able woman who was leading the strike. The women did not deal directly with households, but worked for a number of employers. They went on strike for a shorter day and a larger beer ration, which they must have needed given the thirsty nature of their hard toil. [18] However, Kensal New Town was only tangential to the area of the Mission, which was described as extending over an area bounded by Finchley Road to the East, Malvern and Elgin Roads to the South, Carlton Hill and Finchley Road to the West, and as far as Kensal Green. There is no hard evidence of any substantial Irish population in Kilburn itself at the time.

Why was the church founded ?

On 27 February 1869 the Catholic weekly *The Universe* reported that the temporary church in Quex Road was crowded for the end of a mission. It wrote *"Kilburn will be, in due time, one of the most important, as it is at the moment one of the most promising, missions in the entire Diocese of Westminster."* Yet the writer provided no explanation of why this should be so, and made no mention of Irish people. However, the Oblates' internal publication, in its issue for 1877, published a letter to his superior from Father Arnoux, the parish priest of the new church, in which he discusses his aims, which seem to have included attracting non-Catholics to the Church. In fact, among the earliest Oblates in Kilburn were two converts. [19]

The early days were difficult. Father Arnoux wrote *"It is to be much regretted that, owing to certain difficulties of access, the poor and the Protestants of the district do not dare enter our church."* Looking forward to the future, Father Arnoux wrote in the same letter that as the Catholics increased in number it would be easier to fight against the numerous and powerful sects in the area (by which he meant the various Non-Conformists) who were building "beautiful churches and vast schools". In particular he referred to the Anglo-Catholics or 'ritualists' who had opened schools, orphanages and convents and were in the course of building St. Augustine's, an Anglo-Catholic church of considerable architectural merit in South Kilburn. *The Universe* of 27 February 1869 reported with satisfaction that several families of the 'Ritualistic School' had become Roman Catholics.

South Kilburn

By 1871 the census shows that Irish people were living in multi-occupancy in Alpha Place North, Pembroke Road, Alpha Terrace, Chichester Road, Alexandra Road and Albert Road, which were streets in Kilburn Park, a district of south-west Kilburn which had not lived up to the hopes of the speculative builders who developed the area. Redevelopment had probably driven the Irish population out of other districts. [20] The Irish inhabitants of South Kilburn were mostly labourers, painters and bricklayers. [21] As for the East (now Camden) side of Kilburn High Road, in 1881, Hampstead had 726 Irish-born inhabitants, [22] some of whom may be presumed to have lived in the poorer part of West Hampstead adjacent to Kilburn.

The South Kilburn district was a constant source of complaints by the sanitary authorities and the landlords of the houses. Kilburn was outside the Metropolitan area, and its roads did not drain into the Metropolitan sewers. Stagnant pools of water formed into which decayed animal and vegetable matter was thrown. While Willesden Vestry was willing to adopt the roads, they had first to be put into a reasonable state by the freeholders, who in turn would have to oblige the ground leaseholders to pay the costs. However, if this was done, the ground landlords would be responsible for paying for the unlet parts of the area, and this they were unwilling to do. Yet, until the roads were properly drained, it would be hard to let all the plots, as well as many of the houses which had been built with drainage defects because Willesden Vestry had no district surveyor. A local medical practitioner, Dr Davson, had been told by the Local Government Board in Whitehall that these public health problems were known and that a medical inspection of South Kilburn would be carried out. [23]

South Kilburn houses could not be let at the £60 per year expected by the landlords, who were reduced to letting the houses in flats, which were then sublet in rooms. [24] Witnesses at the official enquiry in 1874, held to decide whether Willesden was to adopt the new Local Government Act, said [25] that the houses in Carlton Road "had to be farmed out to anyone who would take them". In 1869–1870 Willesden Vestry had been obliged to take out 600 summonses for non-payment of rates. This suggests that many of the houses produced insufficient rent. As the Revd George Despard of the Anglican Holy Trinity Church in Brondesbury Road, a well-off part of Kilburn, wrote on 16 September 1867 to the National Society for the Propagation of the Gospel, asking for funds for a school, "more than two-thirds of the whole population of Kilburn consists of the lowest class of the labouring poor of London". [26] Most of the outdoor relief provided by the Willesden District of the Hendon Poor Law Union was paid to inhabitants of South

Kilburn, living in Denmark Road, Pembroke Road, Chichester Road, Carlton Road, Alpha Place, Alpha Terrace, Canterbury Road and Canterbury Terrace. Before new premises were secured for the workhouse in Salusbury Road, there was a local 'workroom' in Pembroke Mews for the obligatory work that recipients of help had to perform. The 1881 census showed a large and spreading poverty-stricken Irish population in multi-occupancy in these South Kilburn streets. The church in Quex Road was their spiritual refuge.

The church and the school in Quex Road

The Catholic Church of the Oblate Fathers in Quex Road expanded rapidly. The *Kilburn Times* of 11 June 1870 referred to a series of special sermons being given by relays of priests.

Fr. Cooke, the founder of the church, claimed that the first important development of the Oblates' mission had been new Catholic schools in Kilburn, "where a new town had suddenly sprung up". The first local Roman Catholic school, established in August, 1868, early in the life of the church, was one of a number of parochial schools set up at the same time as new Anglican parishes were being formed to serve the rapid increase in the poor population of Kilburn. The London School Board's inspector visited the school on 13 June 1871, in connection with an application for a grant to expand the building to accommodate 150 children. The inspector took a poor view. The schoolrooms were in a house and shop. The infants were accommodated in a dark basement, used for cooking after school hours. The ground floor was the shop. The junior boys and girls, who shared toilet facilities (though the applicant, the Revd I F M Arnoux, stated that "only one at a time goes"!), were taught on the first floor. This was obviously a school for the poorest children, given that the fee was one penny a week "for those who can pay". The building was owned by a coal-merchant, Mr Bird.[27] It may have been the shop on the corner of Kingsgate Road and Quex Road which still stocks Catholic religious items but was for decades a coal agency belonging to the local merchant, Mr Cleaver, who was perhaps one of Mr Bird's successors. Not unexpectedly, given the conditions of the school, both writing and arithmetic standards were poor. The inspector could not recommend the award of a grant, but he wrote that the school was in transition and further consideration should be given later when improvements had been carried out.

However, Roman Catholic provision for schools grew rapidly. In 1871 the community bought a printing works called Carlton Hall in Peel Road, South Kilburn, for conversion to a school[7]. By October 1876, Father Arnoux was informing his superiors that three ladies were teaching the children, helped by three assistants. Of the 270 children registered, about half were non-Catholics.[28] Apparently, parents would send their children to Catholic schools if no place was otherwise available, or perhaps if that was all they could afford. By May 1881, a rival Church of England School reported enviously that the Catholic school could provide sufficient places to accommodate 937 children.[29]

The Catholic population of Kilburn had already grown to 600 or 700 by 1873.[30] London's expansion, however, suggested that the number would increase and that the church, which had places for 220 worshippers only, required enlargement. The original building in Quex Road was only 23 metres long by 9 metres broad. The Oblate Fathers lived on the ground floor, while the public place of worship was in the upper storey.[31]

The church of the Sacred Heart would be completed by the end of the 19th century (Fig 2). An account of a bazaar held in Kilburn at that time, which raised £600 in 4 days (an enormous sum, equal to a week's wages of 400 skilled men) to help pay for the work, included no recognisably Irish names[32].

2 Church of the Sacred Heart, Quex Road (begun 1878), in the early 1900s.

Where, then, were the Kilburn Irish? Did their poverty render them invisible, even those listed in the census? The author of an important thesis on the London Irish stresses[33] that 19th-century social description rarely singles them out. Or could it be that Kilburn did not become a notably Irish district until the 20th century and that the very success of the Catholic church in Quex Road was what, among other things, attracted them ?

My sincere thanks to Fathers Ted McSherry, of the Church of the Sacred Heart in Quex Road, West Hampstead, Michael Hughes (archivist of the Oblates), Aloysius Kedl and Michael Coughlan, for their help in tracing archival material.

Notes

1 S Gilley, "The Roman Catholic Mission to the Irish in London, 1840–1860" *Recusant History* 10 (1969–1970) 123–145.

2 J Jackson, 'The Irish in London (London University MA thesis, 1958), Table XIX shows:

Irish-born population	England and Wales (London in parentheses)
1841	289,404
1851	519,959 (108,548)
1861	601,634 (106,879)
1871	566,540 (91,171)
1881	562,374
1891	458,315
1901	426,465 (60,211)

3 See Dick Weindling & Marianne Colloms *Kilburn and West Hampstead Past* (Historical Publications 1999).

4 Kilburn Ward, created in 1873, was the smallest in Hampstead Vestry, with 979 householders and a rateable value of £52, 328.

5 Ref. 2, p 261.

6 Aidan Flood, *The Irish in London* (London Borough of Camden, n.d.), unpaginated.

7 Revd T Collins. "In the Beginning". *Quex Road Review*, Spring 1974, pp 7–11. I thank Aidan Flood and Dick Weindling for bringing this article to my attention.

8 *Missionary Record of the Oblates of Mary Immaculate* (Dublin) 1930, p 175. The original source for this is Ref.9, p 308.

9 Fr. Robert Cooke. *Sketches in the Life of Mgr. de Mazenod, Bishop of Marseilles and Founder of the Oblates of Mary Immaculate*, 2 vols. (London: Burns and Oates, 1879), II, 307.

10 Vincent Denny, OMI, *Reaching Out: History of the Anglo-Irish Province of the Missionary Oblates of Mary Immaculate*, 2 vols. (Dublin: Maromi Publications, 1991) Vol.I, p 75.

11 In the Oblates' internal publication, the *Missions des Missionnaires Oblats de Marie Immaculée* (1866), p 639. The publication is hereinafter referred to as *Missions*. (Translations are mine, M.A.)

12 Ref. 3, p 43.

13 Ref. 3, p.45.

14 Ref. 10, p 175. This point is made in *Missions* (1865), 574 –5.

15 *The Tablet*, 10 May1879; *Missions* (1865) p 575.

16 Ref. 10, p 77.

17 Lyn Hollen Lees *Exiles of Erin*: *Irish migrants in Victorian London* (Manchester UP 1979), p 71.

18 *Kilburn Times*, 29 June 1873.

19 *Missions* (1866) p 639.

20 The phenomenon of 'overflow' from other London districts was being noted by the local press, e.g. *Kilburn Times*, 8 March 1882.

21 I am grateful to Ian Johnson, of Brent local archives, for providing me with lists of Irish-born inhabitants taken from the censuses of 1861, 1871 and 1881.

22 Ref. 2, pp 94–95, quoting Booth's surveys.

23 Several local doctors supported Dr Davson (*Kilburn Times*, 23 March 1873).

24 See the booklet *The South Kilburn Conservation Area* (London Borough of Brent, 1982).

25 *Kilburn Times*, 6 January 1873.

26 Church of England Records Centre, file on Holy Trinity School, Kilburn.

27 Public Record Office, ED 7/88/6 of 21 December 1868, and ED 3/19/20 of 13 June 1871.

28 *Missions* (1877), p 70.

29 Church of England Records Centre, file on St John the Evangelist School. Report to the National Society for the Propagation of the Gospel.

30 *Missions* (1873), p 318.

31 *Missions* (1869), p 473.

32 *Oblate Missionary Record*, Vol. 8 (1898), pp 270–1.

33 Ref. 2, pp142 ff.

Michael Alpert is Professor of the History of Spain at the University of Westminster, and a long-time resident of West Hampstead and Kilburn (see also his article "West Hampstead's Railway Invasion", *Camden History Review* 7 (1979) 16–20).

Camden History Society

The Society was formed in 1970, a few years after the amalgamation of the old boroughs of Hampstead, St Pancras and a part of Holborn, to promote interest in the history of all parts of the London Borough of Camden. Each year it has monthly lectures and outings and it produces a bi-monthly newsletter as well as publications on the history of streets, people, trades and burial places in the borough.

The Society welcomes new members who are interested in receiving the newsletter, attending lectures, going on conducted walks, doing research at different levels, or all of these.

Enquiries about membership should be made to the Membership Secretary, Camden History Society Flat 13 13 Tavistock Place London WC1H 9SH

Gifts and bequests to the Society are always welcome

Camden Local Studies and Archives Centre (CLSAC) Holborn Library, 32-28 Theobalds Road, London WC1X 8PA

CLSAC houses a large local history collection available to the public. The collection includes maps, drawings, prints, rate books, Paving Board records, newspapers, photographs and paintings.

CLSAC also stocks all back numbers of the *Camden History Review* and the Society's other publications, including the Newsletter.

Camden History Society is a registered charity No.261044.

Provident and non-provident dispensaries in Camden

by F Peter Woodford

In my childhood, in semi-rural South Wales, my GP uncle employed a dispenser, who made up the pills and lotions the doctor had prescribed and dispensed them in a dispensary. This gives one meaning of *dispensary*, formerly the same as an apothecary's and nowadays the chemist's (or, more correctly, pharmacist's) shop. In this article, though, which traces the history of public dispensaries in Camden from the 17th century onwards, the term applies to premises staffed by physicians as well as apothecaries, and therefore more in the nature of out-patient clinics. They were exclusively for use by the poor – or at least those too poor to pay a doctor's fee but unable or unwilling to attend the hospital or infirmary if there was one nearby. Some, though by no means all, 18th-century dispensaries also sent their physicians to visit the sick at home, and were therefore more like a modern general practice service; some also provided beds for women in labour, and as a consequence a few became full-time lying-in hospitals.

Until the 19th century, care of the indigent sick was entirely dependent either on the Church or on individuals' benevolence or enlightened self-interest: householders procured medical treatment for their servants not just as a kindness but as a means of self-protection, while those who wished to have their name perpetuated might give funds to build an almshouse, including a stipend for an apothecary to make visits when necessary. Parishes were obliged by the Poor Law Act of 1601 to provide workhouses for paupers, where there would also be occasional medical visitations, often with the aim of preventing epidemics rather than of comforting individual inmates, but workhouses were places of dread (and indeed, often dreadful places) for many who were poor but not paupers.

Medical ministrations at workhouses were paid for out of

what may be regarded as public funds, in that the 'poor rates' levied on householders and landowners in the parish paid for services to the workhouse, though a requirement for health care was not actually specified in the legislation. Some vestries also paid for individual treatment of paupers (considered case by case) outside the workhouse, but this was rare. Not until the Poor Law Act of 1834 was there specific reference to any general system of medical relief for the poor, because of the widespread reliance at that time on private voluntary organisations and philanthropic benevolence.

This article deals only with dispensaries which were independent of hospitals. Several dispensaries came to be established in the 19th century which were under the control and management of a hospital, more what we would call the out-patient department of a hospital, functioning as a pre-admission or post-discharge facility. As Loudon points out in an extensive study[1] of the Dispensary movement in England, it was the disinclination of hospitals to extend their out-patient care into the surrounding community which prompted the establishment of public dispensaries and ultimately led to their flourishing.

18th-century enlightenment

To their credit, the Royal College of Physicians of London opened a public dispensary in 1697, in Warwick Lane, not far from St Bartholomew's Hospital. But its opening had been bitterly opposed by a faction within the College (who saw some of their revenue disappearing if free treatment were to take hold), and after a quarter of a century of continued in-fighting it closed in 1725.

In 1769 a Dr George Armstrong opened the first public dispensary in what is

now Camden, "for the sick children of the poor", the first premises being at 7 Red Lion Square. It seems that this was still an instance of private benevolence, because the entire expense was borne by Dr Armstrong himself. The dispensary soon moved out of Camden, and by 1772 was established in Soho Square. It faded out around 1783 when its founder had fallen into debt. Spare a tear for this example of virtue conspicuously unrewarded.

1770 is an important date: it saw the foundation of the General Dispensary in Aldersgate Street in the City, which served as a model for many another public dispensary. The Aldersgate dispensary was housed in grand surroundings – Dorchester House, built as the town house of the Marquis of Dorchester and occupied later by Lord Shaftesbury, which had also been used as the City of London Lying-In Hospital. Dr John Coakley Lettsom was instrumental in founding the General Dispensary (and incidentally, many other major medical institutions), and he published the principles on which it operated. The General Dispensary was designated Royal in 1849.

In 1774 the Quaker banker Henry Hoare, whose family was later to become famous as defenders of Hampstead Heath, together with a few wealthy friends, founded the Westminster Dispensary for the free treatment of the sick poor.[2] This dispensary covered the vast area of north London not covered by the General Dispensary, namely that bounded by Holborn Bars, Gray's Inn Road, the New Road all the way to the Edgware Road and thence to Westminster Bridge – thus, including all the built-up part of what is now Camden. Its premises were at 9 Gerrard Street, Soho (interestingly, the former Turk's Head Tavern where Johnson, Boswell, Garrick, Goldsmith and Reynolds congregated in

the Literary Club).

By 1792 there were 16 general dispensaries in London (and 22 in the provinces).[1] Only one of these, apart from the Westminster, covered or was in the present Borough of Camden, namely The Public Dispensary, Carey Street (1782; sometimes listed[3] as being in Bishop's Court, Lincoln's Inn). Striking, when one looks at details, is that these were far from being hole-and-corner affairs (unlike Dr Armstrong's): the physicians in charge were mostly leaders of the profession, officers or presidents of the Medical Society of London, the Royal Society of Medicine, the Royal College of Physicians or Surgeons; and often, later, knighted.

Non-provident dispensaries

The first dispensaries were all financed, like voluntary hospitals (e.g. the Westminster, the Middlesex, the London), by *subscribers*, who were then authorised to write letters of 'recommendation' for patients considered to be proper objects of charity. The number of patients a subscriber could have on the books was proportional to the size of the subscription. At the Public Dispensary in Carey Street, for instance, an annual subscription of a guinea enabled the subscriber (who was called a *governor*) to have one patient on the books during that year; a donation of 10 guineas made the donor a Governor for Life, allowing one patient to be on the list constantly.

Thus, these dispensaries were not broadly philanthropic, "open to all, and free at the point of delivery" like the present UK National Health Service. Eighteenth-century donors held fast to the tenet that the poor should be helped, but only the deserving poor. The donors were motivated not solely by altruism, but also by snobbery and ambition[4]: lists of

28   Camden History Review   Vol.25 (2001)

subscribers were published, and it was no disgrace to see one's name listed alongside such luminaries as (again in the case of Carey Street) the Earl of Sandwich, the Earl of Sussex, the Lord Chancellor, the Lord Chief Justice, the Master of the Rolls, the Attorney-General, the Solicitor-General, the Lord Mayor of London and several Members of Parliament, including William Wilberforce.[5]

Attached to each dispensary would be at least one physician, usually several, and one or more surgeons. Dispensaries providing midwifery services, such as the Westminster General, appointed physician-accoucheurs and midwives. The 31-year-old Dr Peter Mark Roget was one of the physicians appointed in 1810 to the newly founded St Pancras (& Northern) Dispensary at Somers Place (126 Euston Road), where his uncle Sir Samuel Romilly, then Solicitor-General under the Regency, was a subscriber. We find a physician-accoucheur attached to the St Pancras Dispensary publishing an article[6] in the first volume of the Transactions of the Obstetric Society of London, in 1859, and it is not surprising to find that he later becomes the president of the Royal College of Obstetricians and Gynaecologists. It was on this self-same site that Elizabeth Garrett Anderson in 1899 located her New Hospital for Women, transferring her female staff from what had begun as a dispensary with midwifery services exclusively for the treatment of indigent women and their children in Seymour Place, Marylebone, possibly displacing the St Pancras Dispensary to Oakley Square, see later.

Provident Dispensaries

During the first half of the 19th century another system of financing dispensaries was introduced. It was first suggested by a Dr Henry Lilley Smith of Southam (Warwickshire) in 1830, and put into effect in Derby.[7] In this so-called self-supporting system, members of the labouring class made small regular contributions (one penny a week for individuals, or twopence for a man, wife and all children under 14 years of age), thereby becoming Free Members. A Free Member was entitled to medical care, including home visits, without charge when it became necessary. For a further contribution of 5 shillings the wife of a Free Member could receive medical or midwifery attention during her confinement, provided the sum was paid 3 months before the expected date of delivery. The income from these small subscriptions paid for all the medicines and appliances prescribed; these were supplied at the physicians' sole discretion, i.e. were not subject to scrutiny by the committee of management. This income stream was supplemented by the donations and subscriptions of better-off local residents (Honorary Members), who contributed to an Honorary Fund which paid for the working expenses of the dispensary.

At the Derby Provident Dispensary there was for the first 14 years a third category, *charitable members*, consisting of the really destitute who could not even afford a penny a week but who were treated gratis on demand, like Free Members. However, this was found to be so open to abuse from claimants who, it turned out, could actually afford the subscription that it was discontinued in 1844, with a dramatic rise in the number of Free Members and the income from them. Provident Dispensaries throughout the country learned from this experience.

These principles, according to an article[8] in the *British Medical Journal* for 1870, were adopted for a latecomer to the Camden scene, the Haverstock Hill and Malden Road Dispensary, noted in that article as "a comparatively young institution". This dispensary must have been much closer to Malden Road than Haverstock Hill, as it was hardly likely to have been in one of the newly built villas on the Maitland Park estate. Did the author of the article - Dr John Ford Anderson, one of the dispensary's physicians - so name it in order to attach to himself the glamour of southern Hampstead rather than the more appropriate West Kentish Town? The article is specific about the costs the Free Members' Fund paid for (medical appliances and drugs, with the exception of quinine and cod-liver oil, evidently the most expensive medicaments at the time) and those for which the Honorary Fund was used (rent, furniture, coals, gas, dispenser's salary, quinine and cod-liver oil).

Objections and problems

A report[9] from the Royal Victoria Dispensary at Northampton, opened in 1845, describes a series of problems which were doubtless common to all the provident dispensaries as they started up.

1 Founding the Dispensary in the first place was opposed by some on the grounds that the provident poor (defined as those who could support themselves by their own labour) were already helped to pay for medical assistance by the various Benefit Societies and Sick Clubs then extant in Northampton, or else they could go to the General Infirmary and obtain a ticket of admission if they didn't already have a subscriber's letter of recommendation; whereas the *im*provident poor, those who were not deserving and respectable but feckless or unemployed, could get assistance from the medical officer provided by the Poor-Law Union. However, experience had shown that reluctance to call in a doctor with the prospect of later facing a bill of unknown magnitude, or inability to attend the infirmary because the illness was too serious, meant that diseases could progress beyond cure or to much greater difficulty in treatment; and if infectious had wider, serious effects.

2 There were of course also doctors' fears that their practice, and income, could be drastically cut if care were provided on a wide scale amongst the poor, who were the most susceptible to disease. These fears were quickly calmed by the reflection that an attending doctor was often unable to recover his fee from poor patients who called him in, and that those appointed as physician to a dispensary could count on a regular salary.

3 This raised another question of policy: how many physicians should there be to a dispensary, and how much should they be paid? In all these institutions, the residue from the Free Members' Fund after the drugs and appliances had been paid for was divided amongst the attending physicians. In what proportions? At first, the physicians were paid in proportion to the number of cases each dealt with. Then it was recognised that some cases involved far more work and time than others, and an attempt was made to categorise or grade them, and weight the salaries accordingly. When this proved too difficult, an ingenious solution was introduced at Northampton which I note had been adopted without discussion at Haverstock Hill 20 years later. Each Free Member was asked to state which of the appointed physicians he would prefer to attend him and his family, and the share of the fund accorded to each physician was in proportion to the number of 'votes' he received (or as it was more blandly put, to the "number of members who enter under each"). Quite an incentive to the physicians to treat patients well and with compassion!

4 As to the right number of doctors to be appointed, the committee secretary of Northampton dispensary (what we might call the *group practice manager*) thought three was about right. Some members of his committee considered that any number who wished to apply should be appointed, but were willing to compromise at six; some of the six who were appointed evidently found that their income from the dispensary (shared amongst six) did not make it worth their while and resigned, so (to the author's satisfaction[9]) the number eventually reached was three, which was found to be the right number for that particular institution. Naturally, the ideal number depended on the size and type of the population served, but a general principle emerged that there should be just enough doctors to cope in reasonable comfort with the workload.

5 Next came the question of who should be eligible to be Free Members. Most people today believe that all citizens have an equal right to free health care according to their clinical need, but the Victorians (like the generations preceding them) had a clear concept that only the deserving poor should be helped through public dispensaries. In this instance the deserving were defined as those with a middling-low income, that is to say employed at a wage enabling them to put in that penny or twopence a week, but not so well off that they could afford to 'go private', i.e. pay a doctor's or midwife's fee when occasion arose. Those who could *not* afford the regular small subscription had to have recourse to the vagaries of the

Camden History Review   Vol.25 (2001)   29

Poor Law or private charity. However, the benevolent shrank from applying a means test to see whether the individual fitted; instead, they pitched on the idea of classifying as 'eligible' men employed as labourers but not as foremen.[9] Labourers still had to make application to be Free Members, stumping up a month's subscription (4d or 8d) in advance, returnable if their application was rejected.

6 Another problem was the existence of what we today would call *benefit fraudsters*. Applications to be Free Members theoretically had to be made when the applicant was healthy; some canny workmen left it until they or a family member was ill, benefited from the treatment while they paid only a penny a week for it, and defaulted on the weekly payments thereafter. This short-term policy was also short-lived, since it did not work a second time. More difficult to spot were those who claimed to be only just able to afford a small weekly payment, though their income actually put them above the eligibility bracket. (There were no grades or classes of treatment by dispensaries, as there are with modern health insurance plans, into which not poor but not rich patients might have been slotted on payment of a higher premium; it took the sophistication of 20th-century entrepreneurship to arrive at these alternative arrangements.)

7 Finally, there were occasional circumstances in which genuine Free Members found it impossible to keep up the payments, modest though they might appear. Late payment was tolerated, but fines were imposed that were proportional to the length of the delay. The books show that fines in some dispensaries could provide as much as a tenth of the total subscription income.

Other dispensaries in what is now Camden

Closest geographically to the Westminster Dispensary in Gerrard Street was the **Bloomsbury Dispensary**, founded in 1801 at 62 Great Russell Street, for which there are good historical accounts by Rona McAuliffe[10] and Gordon Taylor[11]. Its best-known physician was Edward Jenner, who introduced his newly discovered

vaccine against smallpox to Londoners (both rich and poor) from his base here. He lived in one of the new houses in Bedford Place just round the corner. Although he moved back to his country practice in Berkeley, Gloucestershire after a year or two, he remained on the medical committee of the Dispensary until his death in 1823. The Bloomsbury Dispensary was strategically placed to serve the teeming slums of St Giles to the south and the courts and alleyways on the Foundling Estate around Great Ormond Street to the north-east. Although this was a non-provident as well as provident dispensary, the poor wishing to have free treatment had to be known to the vicar of St George's Bloomsbury or St George the Martyr, Queen Square, or, later on, of one of the many other churches in the vicinity (Bloomsbury Central Baptist Church; Christ Church, Endell Street; the Bedford Chapel and the French Protestant Church on Bloomsbury Street) as proof of their comparative respectability. We are still in the realms of the 'deserving poor'. But house visits *were* made (and what an eye-opener they proved, for the attending physician!); 369 of these calls were made in 1933.[12] Bombed in 1941, the Bloomsbury Dispensary moved to Bloomsbury Street. The coming of the NHS in 1948 made its work as a free GP service redundant, but it remains in existence as a charity arranging respite care and accompanied holidays for the disabled poor.

The **St Pancras & Northern Dispensary** at 126 Euston Road, founded 1810, has already been mentioned. Its workload of 7,390 patients treated in 1869[13] exceeded that of the Bloomsbury Dispensary's of 5,278; these were undoubtedly the largest dispensaries in what is now Camden but hardly approached the workload of the Westminster General's 10,632 - which, it must be remembered, had a vast catchment area. The St Pancras Vestry minutes of 17 February 1864 record an appeal of the SPND against the rates being imposed, and the minutes of 20.9.1865 and 3.10.1866 duly record rate revisions to an unstated "minimal sum" (though why this should have to be done in three successive years is unclear: perhaps the Vestrymen's concept of a minimum did not coincide with the Dispensary's subscribers'). Some sources[3] give the

Northern Dispensary's address as "Somers Place, New Road": evidently, the dispensary building stood well clear of the road - as was required in the early days of the New Road - with a 'place' or forecourt before it, which illuminates the complaint in the vestry records for 8.9.1880 about the unauthorised erection of buildings in the forecourt of the dispensary at No.126. In the 1933 survey[12] listing of dispensaries still operating, there appears a non-provident St Pancras Dispensary at 39 Oakley Square; I have been unable to ascertain whether this is the same dispensary displaced by the New Hospital for Women, as suggested above. There was a confusingly, and according to some sources grandiosely named St Pancras General Dispensary or *Royal General Dispensary* at **26 Burton Crescent** (now Cartwright Gardens), south of the Euston Road but strangely close to the St Pancras & Northern Dispensary across Euston Road to the north. Perhaps this was a provident dispensary, as distinct from the better-known non-provident dispensary to the north; certainly the one in Oakley Square is marked as non-provident.

Also still providing a service in 1933 was the **London Medical Mission** at St Giles' Buildings, Short's Gardens WC2, in the vicinity of Seven Dials – an area subject to much-needed missionary work of all kinds.

The only traces of the **Camden Town Dispensary** I have been able to find are in the St Pancras Vestry minutes, in which every two years or so from 1859 there was a request (for years on end by a Dr Bermingham, then for years by a Mr Bermingham, who must have retired or become a surgeon by then) for the use of the Vestry Hall for a "concert in aid of the dispensary in Hawley Crescent" (1859) or "in aid of the Camden Town Dispensary" (1861 and subsequently). From this I deduce, in the absence of further evidence, that these dispensaries were one and the same, as Hawley Crescent is in the heart of Camden Town. The request was always granted. Then on 21.11.1889 there is a single mention in the Vestry records of the grandly named Metropolitan Medical Dispensary, Camden Town – again for the use of the Vestry Hall for a concert in aid. This too might be the very same

establishment; to date I have found no other trace of it or them.

Next we encounter some dispensaries which turn out to be hospital dispensaries. In 1857 came the London Dispensary for Diseased and Ulcerated Legs, founded under Florence Nightingale's auspices at 1 Red Lion Square (harking back to the very first dispensary at No.7). This was *not* a self-supporting public dispensary, and was probably located there because St Paul's Hospital for Skin and Urological Diseases was then in Red Lion Square, though it was soon to relocate to Endell Street. Similarly, the Northern Dispensary, Gower Street[14] (not to be confused with the Northern Dispensary mentioned above) was so called because it was attached to the North London Hospital, founded in Gower Street in 1833 and later re-named University College Hospital. At the Nouvel Hôpital et Dispensaire, Shaftesbury Avenue, hospital and dispensary were joined together in the title, which is still preserved on its rear façade on Monmouth Street, now the front of the Covent Garden Hotel.

Highgate Dispensary was founded very early, in 1787, "for the poor of Highgate, Muswell Hill, Crouch End, Hornsey and Holloway" - thus not in or near an urban rookery but in a charming rural village. However, farm labourers who earned low wages and were often housed in picturesque but insanitary cottages were as much in need of free or almost free medical assistance as people in any crowded slum. The Minute Book of the Dispensary for 1840 significantly records the decision to change its nature, namely that it should no longer be 'free' but "self-supporting, aided by voluntary contributions...So ended the long established Free Dispensary of Highgate, after fifty-three years of useful existence." This must mean that this dispensary adopted the mixed provident/honorary subscribers arrangement described above for the Haverstock Hill and Malden Road Dispensary, and dropped the principle of absolutely free 'charitable members' 4 years before this category was dropped at Derby (which, admittedly, was set up in the first place primarily as a Provident Dispensary). Home visiting from the Highgate Dispensary was provided for in

1 Pond Square, Highgate, c.1850, showing the two ponds and Dr Wetherell, physician to Highgate Dispensary, watering his horse (watercolour by Miss Wetherell). Dr Wetherell's house is in the centre (with two chimneys), the *Gatehouse* to the right. The view is probably taken from the dispensary, which is (as it were) behind the artist on South Grove. [Courtesy of the Highgate Literary and Scientific Institution]

Peter Woodford, not a doctor but a clinical biochemist, has recently been appointed Affiliate of the Royal College of Physicians of London, the first non-medical person to be appointed at Fellowship level since the founding of the College in 1518. He has been this journal's editor since 1995.

the original rules, but only in exceptional cases when the patient was "absolutely incapable of attending"; likewise, the 1787 constitution scrupulously avoided interfering with local midwives, the dispensary physician being obliged to attend a confinement only when requested by the midwife on the case. In 1864 the dispensary premises were in South Grove, adjacent to Pond Square (Fig 1) which at the time contained two ponds plus a lot of drowned kittens and other litter. Dr Wetherell, the attending physician (appointed 1840), was one of those who strongly opposed draining and building on Pond Square at a public meeting[15] in 1864, at which time he and his partner Dr Moger were being paid £20 annually by the dispensary. The last address of the dispensary was 54 Highgate West Hill, and subscriptions and donations were still being recorded in 1928.

New End Dispensary, Hampstead, was founded at No.10 New End in 1845, probably in association with New End workhouse, thus more of a hospital dispensary than an independent one. However, the crusading Revd Thomas Ainger, vicar of Hampstead parish church and chairman of the Hampstead Wells and Campden Trust[16], transformed it in 1850 into a Provident Dispensary at No.*16* New End, where it shared premises with a soup kitchen, another vital resource for the indigent which may well have done more for their health than any medical treatment of the time. I have absolutely no idea why Hampstead lagged nearly 60 years behind Highgate in providing a dispensary. Perhaps the governors of the workhouse suppressed the idea.

Although several authorities, including Loudon[1], maintain that the dispensaries, especially provident dispensaries, became redundant and disappeared after the passing of the National Insurance Act of 1911, the facts - in Camden at least - do not bear this out completely. The Bloomsbury Dispensary is still in existence (see above), donations were still pouring in to the Highgate Dispensary in 1928, the London Medical Mission in Short's Gardens was still functioning in 1933, and the funds supporting the Hampstead Dispensary were transformed into a continuing Hampstead Aid in Sickness Fund in 1953. It was the National Health Service Act in 1948 which sounded a definitive death knell to dispensaries as free general practices, so that those that survive turn to relieving distress associated with ill health or disability instead of providing medical or pharmacological treatment.

Acknowledgement

I am indebted to Ms Pamela Clifton who first aroused my interest in the subject and who did valuable preliminary work on it before other concerns in her life took precedence.

Sources

Wellcome Institute for the History of Medicine
St Pancras Vestry records, indexed by John Richardson (at Camden Local Studies & Archives Centre)
Royal College of Physicians of London (Wellcome Library)
Royal College of Obstetricians and Gynaecologists
Highgate Literary and Scientific Institution
Hampstead Wells and Campden Trust records

References

1 J S L Loudon. "The origins and growth of the dispensary movement in England" *Bull Hist Med* 1981; 55: 322-342.
2 William Hartston. "Medical dispensaries in eighteenth-century London" *Proc Roy Soc Med, Hist of Med Section* 1963; 56: 17-22.
3 J P Griffin "A short history of the dispensary movement in London from 1675 to 1948" *Adverse Drug Reactions & Toxicology Review* 2000; 19: 249-264.
4 Bronwyn Croxson. "The public and private faces of eighteenth-century London dispensary charity" *Med Hist* 1997; 41: 127-149.
5 Records of the Public Dispensary (Library of the Royal College of Physicians of London).
6 (Sir) George Duncan Gibb. "Fatal effects of grief on a puerperal patient" *Transactions of the Obstetric Society of London* 1859; 1: 75-76.
7 John Jones. *Self-Supporting Dispensaries: their adaptation to the relief of the poor and working classes* 1862.
8 John Ford Anderson. "Provident dispensaries: their object and practical working". *British Medical Journal* 1870 (i) 516-518; discussion p 533.
9 John Becke. *Provident Dispensaries: Sketch of the facts connected with the establishment of The Royal Victoria Dispensary at Northampton* 1870.
10 Rona McAuliffe. *The Story of the Bloomsbury Dispensary* Trustees of the Dispensary 1973.
11 Rev Gordon C Taylor. "The Bloomsbury Dispensary, then and now" *Pharmaceutical Historian* 1990; 1: 2-5.
12 *Joint Survey of Medical and Surgical Services in the County of London. Part 1. Voluntary hospitals, clinics and dispensaries.* London Voluntary Hospitals Committee. P S King & Son, 1933.
13 *London and Provincial Medical Directory* 1869.
14 Referred to on p 20 of Barbara Ely's "The obstetric Dr Davis, 1777-1841" *Camden History Review* 1978; 6: 20-21.
15 Joan Schwitzer "The struggle for Pond Square" *Camden History Review* 1975; 3: 6.
16 Christopher Wade *For the poor of Hampstead, for ever: 300 years of the Hampstead Wells Trust* Camden History Society 1998.

Architectural details on Hampstead Houses

by Bryan Diamond

When I moved from Pinner to Fitzjohn's Avenue in 1990, I became fascinated by the wealth of architectural detail on the houses in my neighbourhood, especially those of the so-called "Queen Anne" style[1], mostly built between 1880 and 1914. I found that neither Camden nor London Metropolitan Archives had any collection of these details, and I started photographing many of those within a short distance from my home, often with a telephoto lens (many details are high up, on upper storeys, under eaves or on gables or the roofs of these large houses, and largely unnoticed by the average passer-by; indeed it seems surprising that some were put in place, so obscure are they).

Publications such as *The Streets of Hampstead*, of this Society, and that by Alastair Service give useful information as to builders and architects of some of the houses, Calloway's *The Elements of Style* gives background to various materials and technical terms, and others on glass or tiles include pictures of comparable items. I have largely educated myself by observation as to what is likely to be an original feature. Decorative materials include metal (usually cast iron), wood, ceramic tiles, stained, painted and etched glass, brick, often carved, terracotta, plaster and concrete.

These details show how prosperous clients in this period were able to embellish their large houses with a wealth of detail. Even smaller houses, such as in "no-nonsense" Gayton Road, often have attractive decoration. The decorative items were mostly taken from merchants' catalogues, but some were probably individually commissioned. Early Victorian terraced houses have few details of interest, and after 1918 the style became plainer, although some later houses have nice Art deco glass or sculpture. These contrasts were well surveyed by

the architect Floyd in 1960,[2] although I do not share his view that "after 1870, chaos resulted", with contrasting elements contributing to "an architectural nightmare"; I agree, rather, with most commentators that the eclectic mixture is attractive. It is more profitable to consider and appreciate the changes in architectural taste from classical Georgian to the decorated style I am concerned with, followed in the 1920s by a move towards modern severity.

Most Hampstead buildings are in good condition, although I have seen crumbling stone, modern ventilation punched through decorative panels, and wiring trailed insensitively over facades. Ironwork is, however, particularly vulnerable, and the little railings known as *balconets* that retained flower boxes are often totally or partly missing. Very few of the buildings I have photographed have been officially listed[3] and thus protected from alteration.

It is interesting to see some motifs, such as the popular sunflower (*cf.* Service's book, top of p 7), used in various materials such as brick panels, plaster and iron. I now describe a few of the details I have seen, some illustrated in the accompanying Figures.

Glass and tiles

The Victorians loved stained glass, and medieval themes (see Barrett & Philips[4]). Some of the most beautiful material is the window glass that includes delicately painted panels (known as *quarries*) of flowers or birds, as in Fig 1 (reproduced here in black and white). One needs to choose the right time of day to see such glass well from outside. This decoration could not have been used in the earlier Georgian sash windows. Some windows are made up of many such little panels, e.g. Fig 2 of foliage, flowers and fruit, and sometimes birds are painted on

foliage: these designs show influence of the Arts & Crafts movement. Alternatively, a single large design can fill the entire window, Fig 3. The stained portion of a window sometimes has deep vivid colours.[5] A simple geometric design is sometimes used, the lead glazing bars being part of the pattern[6], and the lead may be used alone for an Art Deco floral motif[7]. Bubbles (*bull's eyes*) are occasionally included to give texture.[8]

A less well-known type of glass, often in a front door, is the etched or engraved variety such as Fig 4. Etched and coloured glass panels are sometimes included in one window[9]. Also colourful are many of the ceramic tiles: sometimes high up in a band below the eaves, of a simple design, probably of the inlaid *encaustic* type, as in Fig 5. These may also be used in small bordered panels lower down the façade[10] or even on a roof pediment[11]. (The medieval style can be compared with those in the Tile Room at the British Museum.) Riotous floral designs are found within porches: good examples survive in smaller houses in Heath Hurst Road and Frognal (Fig 6). The combination of styles is cheerful, but perhaps not now considered in the best of taste. These tiles came from kilns in the Potteries. An elegant rococo band with cherubs, foliage and a basket of flowers, in brown/white, is over the door at 8 Lyndhurst Road.

Tiles were sometimes used for front steps and pathways, usually in a black/white large or small chequered pattern.[12] Tiled hallways were probably common; I have not seen these often, but a good geometrical multi-coloured example is in a small villa in Pilgrim's Lane[13]. Rarely, a mosaic floor survives outside. The best I have seen is at 33 Fitzjohn's Avenue, geometrical and floral in a fan-shaped ground, see part of it in Fig 7.

Brick and terracotta

Warm red brick is the predominant building material in the 1880s Lyndhurst area (earlier a dullish yellow brick is often used, as in Arkwright Road); its decoration takes many forms. A blind Gothic arch is put over a window[14], or beneath eaves a line of bricks is set projecting at 45° as a dog-tooth pattern[15]. There may be one or more lines of brick in contrasting colour - yellow and brown horizontal lines on a darker brick façade on a single villa in Thurlow Road[16], in brown on the yellow façades in Gayton Road[17], and more boldly in brown arcades either around windows or as a small under-eaves frieze at the terrace at 45-55 Rosslyn Hill. More elaborate decoration is in carved or shaped bricks, a small block of raised bricks being sometimes put below a window, which may have a wavy lower border as in Rosslyn Hill and over shops at Nos.2-4, 22 and

1 18 Daleham Gardens, stained glass, 1st floor window (1880s)

2 3 Prince Arthur Rd, stained glass in side door (1870)

3 34 Fitzjohn's Avenue, stained glass in rear stairs, one of two similar panels (c.1880)

4 29 Heath Hurst Road, etched glass in front door (1890s)

5 10 Lyndhurst Road, row of inlaid tiles under eaves (c.1870)

6 26 Frognal, tiles in entrance porch (1880s-90s)

7 33 Fitzjohn's Avenue, part of mosaic entrance path (c.1880)

8 91 Fitzjohn's Avenue, terracotta inset in first-floor brickwork

9 30 Fitzjohn's Avenue, terracotta frieze below eaves cornice (1880-85)

10 1 Nutley Terrace, terracotta panel on first-floor brickwork (1877)

32-36 at the south end of Heath Street. At 27 & 29 Maresfield Gardens, this block is expanded to a larger flower-like design below upper windows[18].

Terracotta panels are widely seen, sometimes coloured to merge with the brick, often with plant motifs, the sunflower being characteristic especially in Fitzjohn's Avenue and nearby, e.g. in a small panel, Fig 8[19], and occasionally used as a keystone in soldier bricks over a window[20]. The flowers may be stylised and difficult to identify: many of them I would designate as "marigold". High up on a roof pediment above shops at 28-36 Rosslyn Hill[21] are panels of marigolds, here made square to fill each small piece. Flowers may be mixed with simple geometrical shapes as in the alternating frieze of sunflowers in Fig 9, or including fruit as in the frieze with a sinuous stem at 37 Frognal[22]. Several small pieces are often used to make a large design, as in Fig 10 at Nutley Terrace, depicting flowers (marigolds?) rising from a pot, all within a high frame; similarly, beside the door at 25 Fitzjohn's Avenue, 14 squares are used to make a tall panel of bold foliage supporting three flower heads, growing from a handled pot.

Larger one-piece terracottas have even more elaborate baroque or heraldic designs, e.g. in Heath Street, with scrolls and a circular heraldic plaque[23]. Swags are often included, as at 47 Fitzjohn's Avenue, 21 Netherhall Gardens, and charmingly suspended by cherubs at 8 Lyndhurst Gardens[24]. A delicate double swag with fruit and flowers tops the white porch (flanked by simple fluted engaged columns, which also have miniature swags) at 4 Lyndhurst Gardens. A black panel at 20 Lyndhurst Gardens bears a swag of fruit and flowers framed with ribbons[25]. An over-door lunette at 53 Frognal has bricks delicately incised with swirling foliage arising from a pot, a flower in relief on each side[26].

The front door is always an important feature, and the surrounding decoration can be very elaborate, as at 22 Lyndhurst Gardens with on each side a swag holding a grotesque mask, foliage and flutings, all surmounted by a large blind lunette. In the impressive doorway in Well Passage, at the side of 17 Well Walk, the large brick/terracotta door surround includes a large keystone, a pair of flanking engaged fluted columns topped by swags, a scrolling plaque, and the date 1884 under a classical pediment[27] – "mid-Victorian eclecticism"[28] indeed.

Terracotta can be used quite sculpturally, as in the bas-relief panel (noted by Wade) at 18 Lyndhurst Gardens, showing a reclining maiden with long flowing hair in Arts & Crafts style[29]. Plaques are popular, in terracotta or plaster. No.10 Arkwright Road has, heraldically, a hart's head upon a shield, amongst scrolling foliage[30]. 1 Arkwright Road has a rampant griffin on a shield, severely set in a circle which is inset in the brick. At 21 Langland Gardens a shield is left blank, surrounded by scrolls which droop below it[31]. Similar blank ovals are seen in the stone carvings over a bay window at 56 Rosslyn Hill[32]. The date of construction may be put in a brick or terracotta plaque, often at ground or first floor level as at 39 Fitzjohn's Avenue, the date 1885 flanking a plain oval amongst foliage and with stout mouldings above and below making a feature of the date. But sometimes it is high up, as on the gable at 30 Heath Street, dated 1889, somewhat crumbling. The date 1878 is over a small window next the front porch at 13 Arkwright Road[33] (higher up is a motto "play and work" upon a scroll; mottoes are rare).

Chimney-pots are rarely decorated, but I have noted the splendid group of nine on 47 Netherhall Gardens. These tall brown cylinders are covered with spirals, net, rosettes or basketwork[34].

Plasterwork

Low-relief decoration *(pargetting)* can enliven large areas of façade. In Fitzjohn's Avenue, Nos.31,33,35,54 & 56 have under their eaves an unusual motif of a daisy set alternately in a double circle and a circlet of leaves (Fig 11). Daleham Gardens is noted[35] for its exuberant decoration, some vividly painted, e.g. Fig 12 with foliage and yellow flowers; the oriel windows have more delicate panels of spiky flowers and foliage[36]. In Maresfield Gardens, Nos.24,26,28 and (adjacent) 32 each have a triangular gable with wild rococo decoration, also in the triangular porch front where, slightly awkwardly placed, is a rectangle with the date[37]. No.32 has further pretty plaster panels in a high frieze extending around the corner onto the Nutley Terrace face.

12-14 Willow Road, at some distance from the Lyndhurst estate, have large panels[38] of a very different style, including many small flowers in a grid with the date 1879, and an almost rococo design of foliage in large swirls. At 26 Netherhall Gardens the oriel panels are bolder, with large and small flowers among foliage (Fig 13). The plaster or stucco can also be incised, as at 93 Fitzjohn's Avenue, with a decorated pot of trailing foliage and flowers[39].

Carvings

There is much high-relief decoration in stucco, cement or stone (it can be difficult to determine the material, especially under paint, when it may be terracotta). Again, front porches often are exuberant. At 16 Fitzjohn's Avenue rectangular capitals to the doorway support a wooden porch roof; these are red terracotta with a small central flower flanked by scrolls and heavy foliage including acanthus leaves, a traditional element. 75 Fitzjohn's Avenue has (under a wooden porch) vigorously foliated capitals to the columns beside the door, while 5 Prince Arthur Road has foliated capitals which extend sideways into the brickwork. 8 Arkwright Road has a pair of arches over the door and a window, supported centrally by rectangular capitals bearing stylised acanthus leaves, but the outer ones have more naturalistic foliage with fruit, apparently apples and pears, the contrast not conforming to classical norms. 16 Willow Road has nice foliage on the columns and in a spandrel over the door (Fig 14). Decoration may surprisingly be put in hard-to-see places; 43 Maresfield Gardens has a shallow lunette over a high dormer gable, with a central shell flanked by leaves and scrolls; such detail needs binoculars to appreciate.

South Hill Park and its Gardens, an "encroachment into the Heath", is a little earlier than the "Queen Anne" style, the bow-windowed brick houses having stuccoed porches with nice stone capitals which are usually foliated (popularised by Ruskin's *Stones of Venice*, 1851). However, a few scattered capitals include heads; at No.11 of the Gardens, male and female cowled winged torsos form the capitals to circular porch columns. The male (Fig 15) has a cross on his chest (is he a monk?) while the female has a tree held beneath her arms - a puzzling pair.

Very detailed foliage fronds form the capitals to square porch columns at 25 Willow Road; 2, 4 & 6 Pilgrim's Lane have various motifs in small over-window lunettes, see the grotesque faces in deep foliage swirls at Nos.4 and 6, but No.2 has apparently a pair of animal heads arising from the foliage, variation indeed in these modest houses[40].

Sculpted heads are found in various positions: at 2 Ellerdale Road a crowned king and queen guard the door[41], in narrow Perrin's Court a smiling boy's head is surprisingly the keystone on a plain early-18th-century house. Perched high on the gable of 26 Lyndhurst Gardens[42] a red terracotta dragon holds a shield and, open-mouthed, stretches his head fiercely forward. Such mythical creatures are rare, but there is another winged creature crouching at the base of the porch pediment, also at 2 Ellerdale Road. Much later in time, at 51&53 Maresfield Gardens, these otherwise plain houses of 1938 are each enlivened by a naked reclining "hefty nymph" (per Wade) in the style of Eric Gill, but the actual sculptor is unknown.

Wood and iron

Decoration in wood is simpler. Bargeboards, when present beneath the eaves, are often decoratively pierced, well seen at 26 Ellerdale Road and 47 Ellerdale Garden, Fig 16; in these, much of the board is cut away; while at 20 Frognal the boards have semicircular recesses near the lower edge, each recess with three radial perforations. At 63 Netherhall Gardens the narrower boards merely have a row of holes, a simple form of decoration, also at 18 Arkwright Road where the same perforations are repeated in the ridged porch. Front-porch structures may have curved supports and sometimes the side of a porch has turned columns (balusters), while at 20 Lyndhurst Gardens the square supports are topped by two large turned balusters. This type of turnery is used, on a smaller scale in a row of eighteen, at the front and side of the

11 33 Fitzjohn's Avenue, curved plaster panel under eaves (1880)

12 14 Daleham Gardens, triangular gable with painted plaster (H. & E. Kelly, 1885)

13 26 Netherhall Gardens, plaster panels under oriel window (1880s)

14 16 Willow Road, upper left part of front door surround, cement or stone (c.1880)

15 11 South Hill Park Gardens, capital to left of porch (1890s)

16 47 Netherhall Gardens, bargeboard (1880s)

17 54 Fitzjohn's Avenue (1880s), side railings above basement area

18 26 Daleham Gardens, railing outside first-floor window

19 104 Fitzjohn's Avenue (late 1880s?), balconet railing at first floor

20 28 Church Row (early 19th century), iron bracket for Windsor lamp attached 1880s

wooden porches in the more modest terrace at 2-14 Willoughby Road[43].

Cast iron became the prime metal material in Victorian days, some hand-made wrought iron being reintroduced later[44]. Despite the widespread removal of railings in World War II many originals have survived in Hampstead (a schedule of railings of architectural interest was prepared by members of the Hampstead Heath & Old Hampstead Protection Society in 1941, and this preserved many gates and railings[45]). From my photos I select Fig 17 as a fair example of scrollwork and pointed finials (Calloway shows several examples of these[46]), cf. the variety of finials on the presumably 18th-century railings in Church Row. In front of some small terrace houses in Willow Road there are good railings; Nos.9 to 11 have twisted uprights with florid terminals, No.11 still having its gate; Nos.15 to 18 are of a different style with bold curving decoration below. Railings beside steps usually have different uprights, in the form of balusters, and two quite elaborate types are used in these Willow Road houses going up to the front door and down to the basement; a similar style was used in interior stairs, cf. Calloway p 261, Fig 6. A little later the style becomes simpler under Arts & Crafts influence: "Ironwork can be quite simple...the sunflower motif was popular in Aesthetic circles"[47] (see Fig 18, here incorporating the sunflower, with a simple rounded finial).

An elaborate example of the low 'balconet' railing mentioned above shown is in Fig 19, a reduced interpretation of full-size railings; it is interesting to see the variety of styles for this simple structure, e.g. rather dense at 27 Fitzjohn's Avenue and a little more delicate at 39 Rosslyn Hill, these having enough connected decoration not to need any upper rail. In Gayton Road those surviving are in the form of a simple rail, decorated only around the supports.

Supports for glass verandas or porches have some of the most elaborate ironwork. I have noted porches at 28 Frognal (with delicate open scrolls), 33 Fitzjohn's Avenue (a deep porch with closer scrolls) and 88 Fitzjohn's (more baroque, recently restored). Some large houses have finials: on a porch such as at 14 Fitzjohn's Avenue, with a pair of crossed rings

below its terminal, or high on a pointed roof, e.g. on the metal-roofed tower at 28 Rosslyn Hill[48], the Gothic villa at 1 Lyndhurst Terrace[49], and topped, above an astrolabe-like structure, with a weather vane on the tower of 55 Fitzjohn's Avenue[50] with different curly finials on the two tiled-roofed towers. Various other surviving iron artefacts can be found if one looks carefully, including a boot scraper in a heavy railing structure at the gate of 21 Netherhall Gardens, a double bell-pull in the gatepost at 6 Gayton Crescent (green corrosion suggests it is bronze) and an open-work hanging bell-pull in a porch in Prince Arthur Road. The lamp bracket at the corner of Church Row and Heath Street, presumably of around 1880, extends into foliage encircling a flower (but not a sunflower!) (Fig. 20).

Coal-hole covers in Camden pavements are described in Vol 23 of this Review,[51] including some in Church Row. The large detached houses in the area I have looked at did not have them, presumably because they had coal stores above ground. But several survive in Gayton Road, Heath Hurst Road (in the front paths) and Belsize Crescent; they are not highly decorated, their patterning ranges from a dozen perforations, criss-cross and dumbbells as shown in Harvey's illustration, to more elaborate radiating patterns, e.g. at 16 Belsize Crescent.

It has been difficult to describe in words many of the architectural details that abound in Hampstead, but I hope to have given an idea of the wealth of surviving decoration which can be seen and enjoyed. I hope it may stimulate readers to walk around these streets and observe, and owners and residents to be even more careful in looking after these features. Copies of many of my nearly 400 colour photographs will be deposited in the Camden Local Studies and Archives Centre.

Sources

Stephen Calloway (ed.) The elements of style, an encyclopaedia rev.ed Mitchell Beazley, 1996.
Bridget Cherry and Nikolaus Pevsner The Buildings of England, London 4: North Penguin Books, 1998 [pp 38, 220-238 and Glossary].
Nance Fyson Decorative glass of the 19th and early 20th centuries David & Charles, 1966.

Alistair Service Victorian and Edwardian Hampstead Historical Publications, 1989 [mainly Walk One].
F M L Thompson Hampstead: building a borough 1650-1964 Routledge & Kegan Paul, 1974.
Christopher Wade The streets of Hampstead 2nd ed. Camden History Society, 1984.
Christopher Wade (ed.) The streets of Belsize Camden History Society, 1991.

References and Notes

1 Led by Shaw and Webb from the 1870s, "a kind of architectural cocktail, with a little Queen Anne, Dutch, Flemish, Robert Adam, Wren and François I" – Mark Girardoux (quoted in V&A leaflet, 1996); and see Cherry, p38 & Service p16.
2 Michael Floyd, "Architecture in Hampstead" in The Book of Hampstead, ed M & I Norrie, 1960, especially pp 124-7.
3 The Statutory List for the London Borough of Camden can be viewed at Camden Town Hall.
4 Helen Barrett & John Philips, Suburban style 1987; The British Home 1840 -1960. Little, Brown & Co, pp 1189.
5 E.g. 8 Ellerdale Road (1870s), in front porch, Art Deco influence.
6 E.g. 33 Daleham Gardens, front door; 6 Well Walk, two front-door panels include textured coloured glass, also in the side of the Food Hall (originally the Express Dairy Company), Heath Street.
7 1 Oakhill Park, in front porch.
8 93 Fitzjohn's Avenue (c. 1878), Perrin's Walk side, bull's eyes spaced in blue stained glass.
9 11 Willow Road (c. 1885), first-floor stairs; etched glass is also found in front doors with pairs of rococo panels at e.g. 15 Willow Road, 28 Maresfield Gardens (this one survives in four similar houses), 108 Fitzjohn's Avenue, 52 South Hill Park, and 29 Pilgrim's Lane (before 1880).
10 51 Netherhall Gardens, brown/white geometric and floral in a black/white border, above windows.
11 23 Willow Road, curved-triangular panel of white and browns in pediment.
12 E.g. 26 Heath Hurst Road, with coal-hole in middle; 26 Lyndhurst Road has large central tiles; 15 Fitzjohn's Avenue with key pattern border.
13 6 Pilgrim's Lane (before 1880).
14 3 Branch Hill (Teulon, 1868); 45 Fitzjohn's Avenue, in contrasting blue and blue/white bricks (1878).
15 58 Fitzjohn's Avenue, above a band of tiles (1880s).
16 Probably early 1860s.
17 1870s.
18 Initialled JW, for builder Julius Wilson, 1884.
19 91 Fitzjohn's Avenue, at 1st floor (1880s).

20 15 & 35 Fitzjohn's Avenue (ca. 1885).
21 Panels of 6 or (on Downshire Hill façade) 12 marigolds on Dutch gables (ca.1880).
22 Under the eaves (1888).
23 Nos.30, 32, 40 Heath Street (1889).
24 Over 1st floor (1880); pediment to doorway (1880s); and rubbed brick frieze over 1st floor (architect Harry Measures, c.1880).
25 Perhaps black terracotta, over ground floor (Measures, 1880s).
26 Opposite UC School; tile-hung frontage, the top bricks of the lunette are chipping; same design is at 55 but painted over (1890s?).
27 Architect Horace Field, who designed several other buildings in Hampstead, including the 1896 Lloyds Bank.
28 Quote from Service p 17.
29 See Streets of Belsize p 78 (1899); cf. Calloway, p 316, Fig 6, relief panel S.
30 Plaster, on chimney breast (1870s).
31 Plaster?, below second-floor window (1880s).
32 Two outer panels of a first-floor window (1890?).
33 Architect Theodore K Green.
34 Large three-storey house, chimneys, in terracotta?, in two rows, of 7 and 2 (c. 1880).
35 Streets of Belsize, p 29.
36 E.g. No.6.
37 Initials JW, for builder Julius Wilson (1884).
38 Panels are evidently of concrete.
39 Panel at 1st/2nd floors, also at No 91 (c. 1885).
40 Lunette over bay window, stone or terracotta .
41 Stone heads in brickwork beside doorway (Green, 1890, DoE listed).
42 Architect Measures, 1886, DoE listed.
43 c.1880
44 Calloway, p 296.
45 A Constant Vigil (100 Years of the Heath and Old Hampstead Society) ed F P Woodford, p 84.
46 Calloway, p 269, especially Fig 6.
47 Calloway, p 333.
48 c.1890.
49 A Bell & J Burlison 1864-5, DoE listed.
50 The Tower, "fine Disneyland Gothic" (Wade), "massive Baronial" (Cherry). Architect J Wimperis, for H F Baxter, 1880-1.
51 A D Harvey, Camden History Review 23 (1999) 89.

Bryan Diamond

was a chartered patent agent, moved to Hampstead in 1990, has researched his family history and written about his 19th-century grandfather's turnery and timber business in Bethnal Green.

History of a late-20th-century development:
Kingswell, Hampstead, 1960–1995

by David Hellings

1 Heath Street in the 1950s, looking up the hill. Buildings up to the end of the white façade remain. (The label on the shop beyond reads Fish, Poultry and Game.)

The original 'King's Well' stood roughly on the site of present-day Hampstead Underground station. It is marked on the map of Hampstead Heath dated 1680, preserved in the Camden Local Studies and Archives Centre. How it got its name is not known: no English king is recorded as having visited Hampstead. Its origin lies well back in medieval times: a *Robert de Kyngswell* is recorded as a free tenant of the manor in 1312, and it seems likely that he took his name from the well rather than gave his name to it. In the 15th century Hampstead High Street was known as Kingswell Street, which implies that the well was the village's main source of water at the time. By the mid-18th century, however, the well appears to have been built over, and the name disappears until its 20th-century revival by the developers of what had been Nos.58–62 Heath Street and 4–8 Back Lane.

After World War II the corner of Hampstead that was to become Kingswell was small credit to the town (Figs 1, 2). A photograph of the corner of Heath Street and Back Lane in 1946 shows it covered in advertising posters. By the 1950s most of the site was occupied by a garage – an inconvenient situation, with very awkward access to Heath Street. The Georgian houses at Nos.60&62 had become seriously run-down, and their Heath Street frontages sported a row of small, unattractive single-storeyed shops. In Back Lane a garage had been built into the back of No.60 Heath Street, and Nos.4–8 were divided into small flats. In the language of the day the site was 'ripe for development'.

Although it was barely 40 years ago, the process by which what was to become the Kingswell site fell into the hands of developers is already shrouded in the mists of history. By 1960 proposals for redevelopment were afoot, and before the end of the year these had crystallised into a plan for one 3-storey and two 4-storey buildings containing 11 shops, a restaurant and no fewer than 45 bedsits, plus a garage for 22 cars. The plan involved the demolition of the two Georgian houses, and was objected to by the then Hampstead Borough Council on these grounds as well as excessive density and "unsatisfactory" appearance. The Heath and Old Hampstead Society, as it then was ((HOHS) also objected. The plan was in fact rejected by the London County Council, but on the comparatively narrow grounds that the density was too

2 Same portion of Heath Street, looking downhill and showing the entrance to the garage in the garden of the Georgian house No.60.

Camden History Review Vol.25 (2001) 37

high and the parking inadequate. The Council's advisers on historic buildings had already expressed the opinion that the Georgian cottages were beyond saving.

The developers were invited to submit alternative proposals, and did so at the end of 1961. The plans had been scaled down to one 4-storey, one 3-storey and one 2-storey building; there were now to be only two bedsits, plus ten 2-bedroom maisonettes, and the garage space had been increased to 29 cars. In January 1962 this plan was given outline permission despite the continued opposition of Hampstead Borough Council and the HOHS, on condition that parking should be for residents only, and that all loading and unloading should be within the curtilage.

It is not known why these plans were not proceeded with, but one may speculate that the developers ran into difficulty in raising the necessary finance. There were no further developments until 1965, when the architect Ted Levy enters the scene. His firm, then Ted Levy Associates, was granted a further outline planning permission in August of that year, by now from the new Camden Council. It was at this stage that the plan for a piazza, instead of conventional frontage development, appeared, but again the proposed development did not take place and it was not until 1969 that things began to move forward.

By this time the site had been acquired by Petty Heath Developments Ltd. They were a subsidiary of a company known as the Property and Reversionary Development Corporation, and they appear to have been set up with the express purpose of developing the Kingswell site. The *Petty* in the name presumably derived from Petty France, where the parent company had its offices. Ted Levy, by now Ted Levy Benjamin and Partners, was retained as architect, and its was his firm that sought and obtained planning permission for the Kingswell development as it was eventually built. The Hampstead Conservation Area Advisory Committee (HCAAC) broadly favoured the proposals and the HOHS appear, rather surprisingly, not to have commented. Nobody seems to have dissented from the GLC Historic Buildings Department's endorsement of its LCC predecessors' view that the Georgian houses were beyond repair.

3 Inside the Kingswell shopping precinct, 1972 (Ted Levy, architect). [Courtesy of British Cement Association]

Levy's Kingswell

Ted Levy's design was indeed dramatic. Not for him the neo-Georgian vernacular or bland brickwork that might have been expected. Instead, there was to be a 4-storey building clad in white with shops enclosing an open piazza on street level (and pedestrian access to Back Lane), more shops fronting onto a pedestrian walkway on the first floor, and offices and eight maisonettes on the second and third floors. Parking spaces had been reduced to 16; the old LCC's strictures in this matter seem to have been forgotten. It was a condition of planning permission that the offices should be for local services. The design, with its white walls and jagged skyline, made no concessions to its Victorian and Georgian neighbours, but stood out as a defiant statement of unrepentant modernism. An abstract modern sculpture, which cost the developers £1500, stood at the foot of the walkway leading to the first floor.

The development proved controversial from the start, but it seems to have attracted little if any criticism on architectural grounds. Instead, argument focused on whether the shops would be too expensive for Hampstead residents, and when the centre was opened by the Mayor of Camden in November 1972 it did so to a protest organised by the Hampstead Village Tenants and Residents Association and led by Labour councillor Enid Wistrich, to the effect that there were too many boutiques and too few shops selling useful goods for local residents at moderate prices. The *Hampstead and Highgate Express* (*Ham & High*) responded with an editorial saying the protest was all very well, but it was unrealistic. Neighbourhood shopping centres were collapsing everywhere, and the future lay with out-of-town shopping centres (a reference to the future Brent Cross). Kingswell would attract trade to the area, and that would benefit other shops as well.

Architecturally, the development received nothing but praise. In granting planning permission, Camden Council observed approvingly that it was "in character with the area". The *Ham&High* editorial referred to above described it as "the finest example of modern architecture Hampstead has seen for a long time" (Fig 3), and Ted Levy was praised for his sense of responsibility. In the same issue of the paper Christopher Gotch enthused: "modern architecture at its most comprehensible ... splendid, in the spirit of Hampstead." The development even made the national newspapers, with praise from John Chisholm in the *Daily Telegraph* for the successful development of "a very awkward site".

To mark the opening, the *Ham&High* printed a 12-page Kingswell supplement which echoed the enthusiasm already shown in its editorial. The paper pointed out that it was virtually the only major shopping development in Hampstead village that century, and noted that the eight 1- or 2-bedroom maisonettes were on offer on 99-year leases at the then formidable sums of between £22,500 and £30,000. This did not prevent their being quickly snapped up. The managing agents alleged that the 18 shop units "could have been let six times over"; nobody seems to have noticed that, ominously for the future, one was empty from the start.

However, any doubts were lost in the general euphoria. The range of shops in the development was certainly striking: there were three boutiques, a restaurant, a pharmacist, a photographer's, shops selling furs, kitchenware, china, glass, lights and shoes. There was a jeweller with its own artists working on the premises, and a Chinese porcelain shop. Enid Wistrich may have had a point with her indignant claim that none of the shops sold useful things for local people, but it must have seemed a wonderful place to come and browse, perhaps buy a birthday present for a friend and end up with a steak in the Garner steakhouse on the corner of Back Lane.

First signs of trouble

In August 1973, when the centre had been open for less than a year, a bomb placed outside the carpet shop went off and damaged it. The bomb had been spotted by an alert passer-by, who had called the police. They had time to clear the area, so there were no casualties. The bomb did not carry the trademark of the IRA, active elsewhere in London at the time, and there was some speculation that it was the work of a local group who had decided to carry Enid Wistrich's criticisms to extremes. But nobody claimed responsibility, and the perpetrators remain unidentified.

Meanwhile, Kingswell settled in as part of the Hampstead scene. For a while all went well, and Kingswell in the 1970s appears to have been a successful retail centre. But by 1980 there were signs of trouble. Although all the units were taken, the eclectic mix had largely disappeared. The jeweller and the Chinese porcelain were gone, and no fewer than seven of the units sold clothing of one sort or another. Another was a shoe shop and another a hairdresser's establishment, and only four (selling cameras, wallpaper, Oriental carpets and adult games) could be said to be the kind of niche retailer for whom the development had been primarily designed. The rate of turnover was disturbingly high.

In May 1983 the centre was acquired by Monseigneur Grills (1983) Ltd (the name was changed to Grafton Securities in January 1986 and to Hague Securities in August 1994). By this time the Kingswell was clearly struggling, and the new owners appointed a fresh architect, Thomas Brent, to review the situation. It was decided to carry out a major programme of improvements, aimed primarily at giving more exposure to tenants at the rear of the development by removing the bridge at the front and carrying out a general upgrade, including replacing the York stone paving by terrazzo tiles, cleaning up the metalwork, improving the lighting and putting seating in the piazza. Ted Levy, defensive of his handiwork, condemned the revamp as "totally unrealistic and unsuitable". But Camden Council raised no objection, and the work went ahead. The opportunity was taken to obtain permission to change the Garner steakhouse into a retail shop and convert the units at the back of the ground floor into a restaurant instead.

The revamp was not a success. The work, which began in January 1984, took longer than expected, and trade suffered. The tenants complained bitterly that after being thoroughly inconvenienced by building work for improvements that they did not want (the terrazzo tiles in particular being criticised as slippery in wet weather) they were faced with substantially increased rents to pay for them. Nor did the alterations attract the hoped-for increase in trade. On the contrary, it seems to have been from around this time that Ted Levy's Kingswell went into a steady irreversible decline.

Ted Levy himself, growling from the sidelines, alleged that it was all the fault of the drive for the highest possible rents, and that if his concept of 'good' shops on the ground floor, with a supermarket at the back and clothing and boutiques concentrated on the first floor, had been followed, all would have been well. But he was being unrealistic. Developers follow the market; they do not follow complex retail strategies that would involve rejecting offers from otherwise suitable tenants and that might or might not work.

Some tenants of Kingswell blamed "ruinous" rents for their inability to make a success of the retail units, and the wallpaper shop – one of the few surviving 'niche' tenants – cited rents as the decisive factor in their decision to move. The managing agents, Ross Jaye, were dismissive, alleging that tenants who failed were either bad managers or in the wrong sort of business. Nevertheless, the number of empty units increased inexorably as the 1980s went by, while other tenants fell into arrears or were forced to pay their rents on a monthly basis. Even the boom years of 1987–9 (and a further round of improvements) failed to halt the trend. By the time the 1990s arrived it was claimed that apart from the estate agents Benham & Reeves, only Whistles Ladies' Fashions (which had replaced the restaurant on the corner of back Lane, with a frontage on Heath Street) and Viva on the first floor (where customers were presumably still attracted by the name) were trading profitably. By the beginning of 1993 12 of the 18 units were empty, the number of burglaries had increased alarmingly, and youths and vagrants were beginning to congregate in the piazza, drinking and using the passage to Back Lane as a toilet. It was feared that the piazza would become a venue for drug dealers. In a final desperate measure the owners proposed converting some of the first-floor units to offices, but Camden Council refused permission.

Proposed solution: a complete redevelopment

Clearly, this could not go on. Grafton Securities decided that only a complete redevelopment would resolve the problem, and invited Thomas Brent to apply his mind to the matter. The design which had won almost universal praise 20 years earlier was now condemned by Brent as "more suited to a Spanish seaside resort than to Hampstead village" and as having "always jarred with the prevailing character of the Hampstead village streetscape". Thomas Brent's solution was to rebuild the ground and first floors entirely, do away with the piazza and passageway through to Back Lane, and reduce the existing 18 retail units to 4, one of which would be a restaurant and all of which would front directly onto Heath Street. Such of the first floor as was not taken up by retail space would be converted to offices, to be accessed from Back Lane, while existing office accommodation on the second and third floors would be converted into three additional maisonettes, with a terrace on the new first-floor roof. At the back of the site there would be a new 3-storey house and two new flats. The storage area in the basement would be removed, providing five extra car-parking spaces.

The managing director of Grafton Securities, Geoffrey Margolis, was aware that these proposals would prove controversial. Although the contrast between the enthusiastic acceptance of the original development and the furore which was to surround the redevelopment 20 years later is striking, it was not due to a lack of sensitivity on the part of the developers. Margolis, who himself lived in Back Lane, strove from the start to win acceptance of his plans by local opinion leaders. He took the view, which may have been exaggerated, that this would be a crucial element in getting planning permission from Camden Council.

Margolis consulted widely. He met with the HOHS in December 1992, with the residents of Kingswell in February 1993 (when the HOHS was represented), and with the residents of Back Lane in February and again in March. The Kingswell residents seem to have accepted the proposals, and indeed remained strangely silent throughout. The residents of Back Lane, despite extensive efforts to woo them and Margolis's agreement to a number of changes to the original plan, did not. They opposed the plans essentially on the grounds that the new residential development would obstruct the view to Heath Street and adversely affect privacy, light and space; they also criticised the enlarged restaurant. The Shoppers Action Committee, the Netherhall Neighbourhood Area and the HCAAC all joined the opposition. Most seriously, the HOHS – which Margolis had particularly wished to win over – was split over the issue.

From the developers' point of view, all seemed well at first. In particular, David Christie, chairman of the HOHS Town Committee, was enthusiastic and prepared a draft report for the Society welcoming the scheme. He acknowledged that the size of the proposed restaurant was a cause for concern, but felt this was outweighed by other advantages. In May he went out on a limb to defend the scheme in an article in the *Ham&High*, criticising the current Back Lane elevation as "ugly and hostile". The proposed redesign would he felt soften the edges of the existing development and integrate it with the surrounding landscape.

Rows over the new proposal

Christie and Margolis were in for a rude awakening. At the HOHS's AGM at the end of June, to which the latter had been invited, speaker after speaker criticised the new development – often, Margolis complained, raising points not previously put to him. If the critics were a minority they were a vocal one; their criticisms centred largely on the size of the restaurant and the disturbance it might cause. Margolis argued that it would at least be of a better class than Macdonald's just round the corner in the High Street or Fat Sam's (a US theme restaurant then occupying premises opposite Kingswell and widely regarded as an eyesore), but the critics were not appeased. No consensus was reached, and the Society faced a difficult task in reconciling the opposing views when drafting their official comments on the scheme. The Society's constitution did not permit the expression of minority views.

The HOHS letter to Camden Council in July was a masterpiece of ambiguity. In principle, the HOHS welcomed "a scheme of improvement", carefully not committing itself to any particular scheme. It acknowledged that Kingswell had never worked as a shopping precinct, and criticised – one might think, a little belatedly – the design of the Heath Street frontage. The proposed continuous frontage would be an improvement, as would the redesign in Back Lane. Some criticisms had been met, and the developers were praised for their scrupulous consultation. But "our strongest reservation is the very significant increase in restaurant space in a street which is already over-supplied with restaurants". The HOHS solution was to restrict the size of the restaurant to that of the existing one, and ban takeaways. By implication, if these criticisms could be met the HOHS would be supportive; but the letter did not go so far as to say so.

In September, Camden planning officials prepared a report to the Planning, Transport and Environment Committee. They summarised the objections that had been made, including those of the Back Lane residents, but there is no indication of how much weight they gave to them, and their main criticism was the alleged loss of a third of the available retail space, blithely ignoring the fact that 12 of the 18 retail units were empty. The residential development at the rear of the site was criticised as conflicting with the service needs of the rest of the development and blocking the view of the residents of Back Lane. More generally, "the visual bulk of the proposal would have an adverse effect on the character of the conservation area".

Camden followed the advice of its officials and refused permission. Margolis claimed bitterly that it was the rift in the HOHS which had caused the rejection, and a disappointed David Christie alleged that the application had not been given a fair hearing because of the "orchestrated and ill-informed campaign against it". In fact, both Christie and Margolis greatly overestimated the influence of the HOHS, and it seems clear that the proposal was rejected primarily on planning grounds. The row within the HOHS continued to simmer in the Letters

pages of the *Ham&High*, and Peter Gorb, then Chairman of the HOHS, found it necessary to write to Camden Council defending the Society against "inaccurate" reports of its views in the local press and emphasising that the HOHS actually opposed the proposals – which must have baffled the Council in view of the terms of the Society's letter in July.

Grafton Securities appealed. The appeal, heard in February 1994, lasted 3 days. Over 100 documents and a score of plans were submitted. The Council argued that the proposed development was contrary to the established policies of the Borough Plan, that the enlarged restaurant would have an adverse effect on local amenities and that the loss of the piazza would adversely affect the building's appearance and the character of the Hampstead conservation area. This view was enthusiastically endorsed by the HCAAC, whose chairman considered that the existing Levy development "closes and completes the view from The Mount in a totally satisfactory manner"; he had particular praise for the piazza as preserving "a 200-year historical reference". He added that the proposed new Heath Street frontage "would be quite at home on Oxford Street but is totally alien to the character and scale" of the Hampstead Conservation Area, and hinted that units were difficult to let because the rents (details of which had not been revealed) were too high.

The developers responded forcefully. Andrew Jaye, partner in Ross Jaye, painted a vivid picture of the commercial decline of the centre through a detailed rental history of each of the units since the present owners acquired the site. The basic design, he said bluntly, had created a retailing disaster. He made the telling point that it had become impossible to let the vacant units even to charity shops at zero rent. So far from the piazza being a local amenity, it had become a congregating point for undesirables which had forced the restaurant to employ a security guard. Thomas Brent weighed in with criticisms of the basic design of the original development ("alien elements of Alicante vernacular") and emphasised the maintenance problems associated with the site, which required a full-time caretaker, which the proposed redevelopment would not.

The developers also pointed out that the Council's calculation

of loss of retail space was flawed. It included space in the basement which was not used for retail purposes. In any event, regarding the shops at rear ground floor and first floor levels as part of the Council's "core frontage" was unrealistic. The developers were more defensive about the restaurant, which was essential to the commercial viability of their proposals. They accepted that it would be larger than the existing restaurant, but denied that this in itself would cause amenity problems, pointing to the advantage to Back Lane residents of the closure of the through passageway from the piazza, an advantage those residents seem to have failed to appreciate.

Meanwhile, the rift in the HOHS remained unhealed. Officially, the Society decided not to give evidence. But two members – Pamela Shipkey and Carol Kenyatta – broke ranks and gave evidence against the developers, the latter going so far as to send to the Council a 4-page letter detailing her objections. This provoked David Christie into giving evidence in favour of the proposal, despite having signed the Society's letter of July 1993 which had so carefully avoided taking sides. The contrast in views was stark. Ted Levy's design, which Pamela Shipkey described as "elegant, ingenious, considerate and neighbourly" became for Christie "a nasty dark gloomy sort of place"; he added the opinion that "the proposed scheme integrates Kingswell with Heath Street". Afterwards, the president and vice-president felt it necessary to try to put the record straight in the columns of the *Ham&High*, by implication criticising those who had spoken at the enquiry. The proposed scheme, they said, was "fatally flawed": not words the Society had used in its letter of the previous July.

The Department of the Environment's planning inspector gave his decision in May 1994. The decision letter ran to 11 closely argued pages, in which the views of third parties were summarised in a single paragraph. Over half of this paragraph was devoted to the evidence of the HCAAC, perhaps because of its semi-official status. The views of the HOHS, despite the furore they had created, received only a single sentence which said nothing about the splits in the Society but stated, presumably on the basis of David Christie's evidence, that the Society "generally supports the appeal proposal in terms of

its design and concept" – precisely what the Society's letter of July 1993 had avoided doing.

The planning decision

The planning inspector identified three issues: whether the scheme would undermine the vitality and viability of the Hampstead District shopping centre, whether the proposed restaurant would lead to unacceptable loss of amenity, and whether the proposal would help preserve or enhance the character of the Hampstead Village Conservation Area. On all three issues he found for the developers.

1 He agreed that the centre was not a viable retail facility as it stood and that the Council's calculation of loss of retail space was flawed, so that far from undermining the core shopping frontage the scheme would strengthen it.

2 He considered that the new design would minimise the impact on the residents of Back Lane and the occupants of the Kingswell maisonettes, while the existing number of restaurants in the area meant that the scheme would be unlikely to have significant impact on the overall level of activity.

3 As regards the third issue, the inspector trod more cautiously, conscious no doubt that he was dealing with an area of aesthetic judgement on which contrary views could be held. He pointed out, however, that Kingswell's contribution to the character and appearance of the area could not be divorced from its economic viability. He did not accept that the merits of the existing development were such that improvement was impossible and, boldly venturing an aesthetic judgement of his own, offered the opinion that the lower floors of the centre were not in fact in keeping with the inherent character of Heath Street. The proposed redevelopment would provide a more acceptable façade (so much for HCAAC's jibe about Oxford Street).

Subject to various detailed conditions, including a midnight curfew on the restaurant, the appeal was accordingly allowed.

End of the story

The story of the Kingswell development actually ends here, for the name no longer applies. Grafton Securities changed its name to Hague Securities shortly after the appeal decision and dropped *Kingswell* as "irrelevant to the current development". (Was it coincidence that the DoE's planning inspector's name was Hague?) Geoffrey Margolis moved out of Back Lane, saying he "felt like a pariah". Pamela Shipkey pronounced her epitaph on the old Kingswell: "Hampstead will be a marvellous place to come to but hell to live in". David Christie riposted that he could not imagine how anyone could find a good word to say about Kingswell in its present state.

In a last-minute change of plan the developers proposed a reduction in the restaurant area and an enlargement to the recessed entrance from Heath Street to provide a sort of mini-piazza where people could eat and drink in the open air, and this was approved.

Work began very quickly after the success of the developers' appeal, and the new development (Fig 4) was open in time for Christmas 1995. But this time there was no mayor, no ceremony. For better or for worse, Ted Levy's imaginative and original design was gone for ever.

Sources
Hampstead & Highgate Express files.
London Metropolitan Archives.
Camden Council archive.

David Hellings lives on Holly Mount, high above Kingswell.

4 The present complex (1993). [Copyright owner sought without success]

Keeley House (*Keeley Street*) and its predecessors

by Geraldine Charles

The impending demolition of Keeley House on Keeley Street off Kingsway – one of three buildings owned and used by the City Literary Institute – and erection of a single new City Lit building on the site sparked my interest in researching and recording the history of this small area of land in what is now Camden.

St Giles, Saxons and lepers

Since the mid-1980s archaeological excavations in the vicinity of Covent Garden, Short's Gardens and Kingsway have revealed that after the abandonment of Londinium by the Romans in 410 AD, an Anglo-Saxon port, Lundenwic, grew up to the west of the old city, having its centre in the Covent Garden/Strand Area. It has been suggested that Lundenwic covered an area stretching from what is now Ludgate Circus to the bend in the Thames at Charing Cross, also spreading north through what became Covent Garden on the axis of Aldwychstrate (later Drury Lane), which joined the old Roman Road of High Holborn. The Keeley House site is located in an area that lay east of Aldwychstrate. Aldwych means 'Old District' or 'Old Port'.[1] Later corruptions are Old Wych or Old Witch.

During King Alfred's reign Lundenwic came under attack from the Vikings and was largely abandoned in favour of the old Roman walled city, which was more easily defended. By 969 AD Lundenwic had passed into the ownership of the Benedictine Abbey of St Peter, Westminster.[2,3] It can be inferred that this included the land that Keeley House now stands on.

During the 12th century Queen Matilda (wife of Henry I) established the Leper Hospital of St Giles, from which the parish of St Giles-in-the-Fields took its name. The parish included today's Lincoln's Inn Fields, Seven Dials and Covent Garden. During the Reformation, the Hospital lands in London became Crown property. Henry VIII subsequently divided the property of St Giles into a western part, given to Sir John Dudley (Lord Lisle), and an eastern part allotted to Sir Thomas Legh. (For the history of the Leper Hospital and the St Giles parish see references 4, 5 and 6.)

Aldwych Close (Old Witch/Wych Close)

(For a detailed account of Aldwych Close see references 5 and 7.)

The eastern part of the St Giles parish was still in the possession of Sir Thomas Legh during the early part of the reign of Elizabeth I. Legh's property included an area known as Aldwych Close. It comprised an 8-acre field bounded to the north by a Close known as Rosefelde, to the south by the '*gardyn of Drurye House and the Close of William Hollys*', to the east by Dalcona Close and to the west by a lane from '*The Stronde to Saynt Gyles*'. Its northern boundary was a common footpath, described in some sources as a private royal road, which was developed (1604-58) to form Great Queen Street. Legh's property, including Aldwych Close, was later inherited by his daughter Katherine Mountjoy. In 1566 the Mountjoys sold the land to Richard Holford. By the end of Elizabeth's reign the name had been corrupted to Oldwick (Oldwych or Old Witch) Close.

During the 17th century Oldwick Close was subdivided, and for the first time the area that would become the Keeley House site begins to be delineated. Of particular interest is the part of Oldwick Close which in 1629 is described as comprising 2 acres bounded to the north or Queen Street side by a ditch, to the east (Lincoln's Inn side) by a common sewer, to the west (Drury Lane side) by a ditch or mud wall and to the south by a ditch or fence, dividing it from the southern part of Oldwick Close which had been leased to John Ittery. Richard Holford sold the 2-acre portion of land in 1629 '*to Sir William Cawley and George Strode in trust for Sir Edward Stradling and Sir Kenelm Digby*'.

To separate Digby's and Stradling's land a wall was erected in Aldwych Close running parallel to Great Queen Street, 197 feet from it. The wall ran northeast from what is now Wild Street towards Lincoln's Inn Fields. Pacing 197 feet from Great Queen Street down Wild Street towards Keeley Street brings one to Wild Court and suggests that the Digby/Stradling boundary wall ran along its present line.

Digby's land lay northward of the boundary wall, between it and Great Queen Street. Stradling's land on the southerly side of the wall and included the part of the Aldwych Close that had previously been leased to John Ittery.[8]

On 27 March 1630 both Stradling and Digby petitioned for licences '*to build a house with stables and coach houses in Old Witch Close, bought of Richard Holford, and lying on the east side of Drury Lane*'. The Attorney General granted the Licences, but the Survey of London[5] found no evidence that Digby built a house in Old Witch Close.

Stradling began building a mansion and on 12 December 1632 he purchased his part of Aldwych Close outright from Calley and Strode. He also subdivided his land with yet another wall, this one running parallel to the Digby/Stradling wall and 132 feet from it, which would put it roughly midway between modern Keeley Street and Kemble Street. On the 20th of the same month Stradling sold the land lying between Digby's wall and the new wall (on part of which Keeley House now stands) to George Gage, the sale including his incomplete mansion, Stradling House. The house is thought to have been completed in 1634. Gage died in 1638 and the house and other property were bequeathed to William Darrell and William Bierly to sell in settlement of his debts; it was purchased in 1639/40 by Humphrey Weld. Stradling's land lying on the other side of the new wall was sold to a Dr Gifford.

Humphrey Weld and Weld House[4,5,7,9,10]

The Weld family came from Lulworth in Dorset. Humphrey Weld was the son of Sir John and Dame Frances Weld and grandson of Sir Humphrey Weld, Lord Mayor of London.

In 1649 Weld purchased Gifford's land and assigned it to his mother, who reassigned it to him 3 years later. By 1652 Humphrey Weld held all the land formerly belonging to Stradling, and he began to build. It is reasonable to assume that when Weld bought Stradling House he applied his own surname to the building

At some point between 1640 and 1657 Weld decided to extend Weld House, apparently to create a residence suitable '*for State purposes, such as the*

1   Enlarged portion of Hollar map of the surroundings of Drury Lane. The unnamed street running diagonally across the view is present-day Wild Street; the two large houses side by side (*arrow*) are presumably Weld House (formerly Stradling House) on the left and the Ambassador's house (on the right).

accommodation of Princes and Ambassadors in London'. In Hollar's map of c.1658 (Fig 1) two large, adjacent buildings are shown fronting on what is now Wild Street (indicated by the arrow). A source quoted by Grey[4] describes Weld House as *'having a centre with two wings, a street front of 150 feet, and a depth behind, with the garden, of 300 feet'*. This description fits the more northerly building (to the left), which is therefore likely to be the original Stradling House that was renamed. The more southerly, rounder building was probably the ambassadorial residence. The term 'Weld House' is sometimes used to encompass both the old Weld House (Stradling House) and the new Ambassadorial residence. The properties passed out of the ownership of the Welds in 1680, when they were purchased by Sir Edward Atkins.

Destruction of Weld House

In 1688 the political situation surrounding James II, his heir and his Catholic Queen (Mary of Modena) reached crisis point. In November William of Orange, James's nephew and son-in-law, landed in Torbay with his army and marched on London. On 10 December the Queen fled to France with her son, the King following the next day. As the news spread, feelings in London were running high; a mob gathered intending to wreak vengeance on *'papists and popery.'*

A new Mass-house in Lincoln's Inn was pulled down and burnt. The mob, which included apprentices as well as some *'villanous thieves and common rogues'* then proceeded to Weld House, the residence of the Spanish Ambassador, the Catholic Don Pietro Ronquillo. The crowd chanted their intent that the fires should not be quenched until the Prince of Orange arrived in London. The chapel of Weld House was ransacked and the ornamental interior, books and manuscripts were burnt. Still not satisfied, the mob turned its attention to the house itself. One observer recorded *'there were thousands of them on Wednesday at the Spanish Ambassador's, they not leaving any wainscot withinside the house or chappel, taking away great quantities of plate ... much money, household goods and writings'*.

Some wealthy Catholics had unluckily assumed that the Ambassador's residence would be more secure than their own and had sent their money and other valuables there for safety. Macaulay states that *'the rich plate of the Chapel Royal had been deposited at Wild House, near Lincoln's Inn Fields'*. The Ambassador escaped with his life and fled to Whitehall Palace.

It is difficult to evaluate from the various accounts the exact state of the house after the riots. The *London Gazette* of

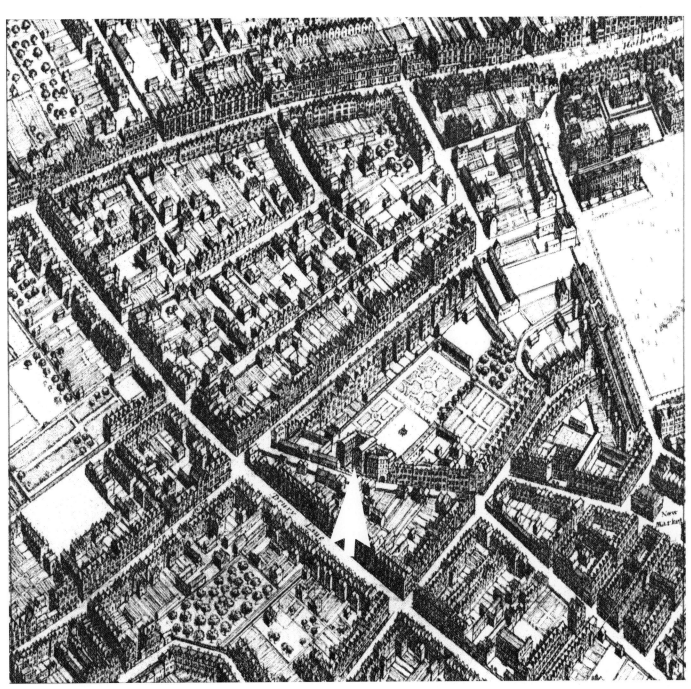

1694 carried an announcement that *'Weld House is to be let, containing 33 rooms, garrets and cellars'* implying that it was habitable, but another account states *'the ruins of Weld House were cleared in 1695 and the land was let on a building lease to a plasterer, Ralph Lister, who was financially assisted by Isaac Foxcroft.'*

Weld House Chapel[11,12]

The Weld House Chapel is said to have been 'erected in 1665 for the use of the Portuguese Ambassador'. It was described as *'a good brick building of an oblong form, with three galleries and a vestry'*. After the riots of 1688 it appears to have been unused until 1699. In 1693 the Baptists had set up a new church in the Covent Garden area. Initially the congregation was under the ministry of John Piggott, but his Calvinistic principles led to a schism amongst the brethren. In May 1699 Piggott and his supporters sought alternative premises and leased the nearby empty Weld House Chapel. The Chapel was in use as a Baptist meeting house from 1700 until 1787, when it was pulled down and a new meeting house was erected on its site and that of the adjoining property. The new larger meeting house opened in 1788 and stood between Nos.23 and 24 Little Wild Street (now Keeley Street). In 1824 the vaults under the Meeting House were converted into a cemetery. From 1874 the St Giles Christian Mission had use of the premises.

Site of Weld House and chapel relative to Keeley House[5,9,13]

Keeley House stands within the precincts of the original Weld (Stradling) House and its grounds. Archaeological excavations in 2001 under the main Keeley House building found evidence of walls remaining from the Weld House complex.. The enlarged Weld House is known to have had a frontage on Wild Street of 150 feet. It probably stretched from the vicinity of Wild Court, along Wild Street and across Keeley Street towards Kemble Street. The buildings and garden also extended for 300 feet northeast, along the axis of Wild Court and Keeley Street. Woollacott[12] writes *'when Mr Piggott and his friends removed to Wild Street, Weld House had been taken down and fourteen brick houses were erected on the site'*. The description of Wild Court below has it comprising 15–16 houses, which suggest that Weld House extended over the site of Wild Court in the direction of Great Queen Street.

In c.1690 a new road was created in what had been the garden of Weld House. Originally named New Weld Street, it later became Little Wild Street and finally (1905) Keeley Street. If the ruins of Weld House were still extant in 1695 (the *London Gazette* quotation above), the new road must have run between the ruins and Weld House Chapel. It is possible to pinpoint the position of the Weld House Chapel, as the 1788 building that was partially built on the Weld Chapel site appears on a number of 18th- and 19th-century maps and is visible in a photograph taken in 1906 (Fig 2).

The St Giles Rookery[6,10,14]

Even in the 17th century the St Giles area had a higher proportion of poor families than the surrounding districts. However, it was during the 18th century that *'its descent into squalor was as rapid as it was spectacular'*. Houses originally designed for single families, but long since abandoned by the class they were built for, were subdivided for letting and sub-letting, while the gardens and open spaces were built on. In their place arose a labyrinth of crowded courts and alleys criss-crossed by narrow pathways, forming what would become known as the St Giles Rookery. The increasing population of the area had various origins. By 1851 rooms could contain anything from 8 to 40 people. Sanitation was virtually nonexistent and the rate of child mortality and infanticide high. By 1861 Church Lane, Short's Gardens and Wild Court were particularly notorious.

The Wild Court Rookery[17]

The grounds of Weld House had rapidly been transformed into *'a congested area of filthy hovels, into which drifted the derelict and foul debris of the social wrecks which can be found in the surging scum of a great city and few districts in the eighteenth century provided so large a reservoir to receive the contagious stream of human impurity that flowed into it, as the parish of St Giles in the Fields'*.[15]

Many of the occupants of Wild Court derived a living as labourers, hawkers, costermongers or street traders. Morley[15] suggests that the Wild Court Rookery originally contained 15 or 16 houses built as supplementary chambers for the Lawyers of Lincoln's Inn. By 1854 the buildings were officially tenanted by 200 families plus *'an unlicensed crowd that nestled at night on the stairs – a thousand people. . .illegal tenants, miserable*

2 Little Wild Street (now Keeley Street), 1906, looking northeast towards Kingsway. Great Wild Street Board School (present Keeley House) is on the left, and the Baptist or Mission chapel is the building with two pedimented doorways further east on the right.

creatures who at nightfall crowd into them and take possession'. Within the parapet of the upper rooms was an open sewer, while inside the rooms ran a trough which was virtually an open drain. Underneath each house was an unpaved cellar, opening on to the court, which was used as a receptacle for garbage.

A view of Wild Court from Wild Street prior to the cleanup of 1854-55 is shown in Fig 3. All the buildings on the right of the alleyway stand on the Keeley House site. In 1854 13 of the houses in Wild Court were purchased by the Society for Improving the Condition of the Labouring Classes and converted to accommodate 100 families (300–400 people) in 108 rooms. Morley[16] gives a description of the Wild Court residents during an official visit by the Society: *'the aspect of the fixed population was not hopeless. There were thoughtful faces, kindly faces and there was not one repellent word or look…The rags hung upon poles from many upper windows like triumphal banners [see Fig 3], the occasional festoons of hareskin, the faces of the young girls looking down with favour on our small procession. . .The strange men with clean faces were indeed gazed at with quiet and perplexed wonder rather than watched with intelligent interest and sympathy; but they had a known right to be there for they represented a society that had bought the property.'* A far cry from the other descriptions of the denizens the St Giles Rookery quoted above.

During the rebuilding Morley reports *'there were more cesspools than houses, 16 to the 13 houses, some of them 16 feet deep and 5 feet square. Out of these before they were filled in [were] taken 150 loads ... in addition, from under the same houses there were removed 330 cartloads of accumulated filth collected in the basements and elsewhere, including vermin'.*[16]

After the conversion, over half the tenants are described as being costermongers, shoemakers and tailors. Those with larger families or better means occupied two rooms. To keep the population of Wild Court in check, rooms were not willingly let to families numbering more than four, and no tenant was allowed to keep lodgers. Each floor had a little gallery with a tap over its own drain which was separate from the water closet and a 'shoot' through which dust and refuse were discharged to a covered bin. Railings on each floor and a common back yard had replaced the drying poles. There was now a superintendent who lived on site, who had access to all the apartments and the right to interfere for the preservation of the property. By 1881 the Keeley House site (the area bounded by Wild Court, Great Wild Street and Little Wild Street) contained 28 individual dwellings and a cowshed.

Great Wild Street School[18]

In the early 1880s it was decided to establish a school on the land bounded by Wild Court, Little Wild Street (Keeley

3 Wild Court seen from Wild Street, c.1850.

Street) and Great Wild Street. A plan of the dwellings and details of the owners and occupiers of each of the properties on the site was drawn up on 30 November 1881 by the architect of the London Schools Board (LSB), Mr E Robson. In 1883 the Eagle Works in Hackney tendered for the contract to erect a school to accommodate 973 children on the Little Wild Street site at a cost of £10,892. The site was officially purchased on 3 April 1884. The problems experienced by the LSB in acquiring the different properties are documented in their published minutes. Robson probably also drew up the final plans for the school, as he remained the LSB architect until 1884.

Great Wild Street (Elementary) School opened on 5 January 1885 under the Headmastership of Mr J Jackson, assisted by a Head for Girls (Miss E G Fernée) and a staff comprising four male teachers and five female teachers plus a teacher for the Infants.

In 1909/10 there were 600 pupils in the Upper School and 358 in the Infants, but by 1924/25 there were only 296 pupils in total, 96 of them Infants. The pupil numbers then seem to remain fairly constant, the last figures available for the school showing only 312 pupils. As no original records of the school are currently traceable, the reason for the fall in numbers of pupils can only be guessed at. It may reflect the general decline in numbers of children in the area resulting from the clearance of slum tenements and the replacement of residential housing with shops and offices.

The date of completion of the school building, 1884, can still be seen carved on the lintel of the disused street entrance from Wild Street. The original name of the school is still (in 2001) visible on the Keeley Street side in the following fragmentary form:
S B[oard] GREAT WILD ST SCHOOL

Although the school closed in 1935, the buildings have continued to be used for educational purposes up to the present day.

Wild Street Centre

From 1936 the vacated school premises were used as an LCC Handicraft Centre until 1947, when the Kingsway Evening

Institute (later known as Kingsway College for Further Education) used some of the buildings. By 1970 only Kingsway College occupied the site, and the LCC's management of the premises had passed to ILEA. In 1974 Kingsway College moved to Gray's Inn Road and the buildings were altered for use by another of ILEA's adult education centres, The City Literary Institute.

Keeley House (The City Literary Institute)

Keeley House first appears in The City Lit prospectuses in 1970–71, when the Department of Music moved into the Keeley House Annexe, the building fronting the Wild Street end of the site. In 1971 ILEA decided that the main part of Keeley House should be adapted as a Centre for the Deaf. This became operational in 1976. Its official opening by Jack Ashley MP on 23 June 1977 is commemorated by a plaque inside the building.

Origin of the name Keeley Street and Keeley House

From the 17th century until the end of the 19th century the name Weld (or Wild) was closely associated with the site. The name Keeley first appears in 1905, when some of the roads in the vicinity were renamed after the construction of Kingsway. Little Wild Street became Keeley Street, being named after the 19th-century comic actor Robert Keeley, the name Weld surviving only in corrupt form in Wild Court, Wild Street and for a time, in the name of the School.

Robert Keeley was born 1793/4 at 3 Grange Court in Carey Street, Chancery Lane. Initially he worked as an apprentice to the printer Luke Hansard, but he relinquished the publishing trade for the stage. He made his debut on Covent Garden boards as Darby in *The Poor Soldier*. He subsequently played in several farces in many London theatres, including the West London Theatre, The Olympic, the Adelphi, Sadler's Wells, the English Opera House, Drury Lane and Covent Garden. In 1844 Keeley and his wife, the actress Mary Anne

Goward, joined Madame Vestris's Company. In the same year he become manager of the Lyceum Theatre and in 1850 joined Charles Kean in managing the Princess Theatre. After two seasons Keeley retired from the stage. He died on 3 February 1869.

The future of the Keeley House site

Keeley House is due to be demolished to make way for a new building to house all City Lit classes. Two archaeological digs were carried out by the Museum of London Archaeological Survey (MOLAS) during 2000. Evidence of Anglo-Saxon occupation was found as well as the remains of walls thought to be part of the Weld House complex. ***Phœnix de cineribus orietur.***

Notes and References

1 Museum of London *The City Literary Institute, Keeley House* Museum of London 2000
2 John Richardson *Covent Garden Past* Historical Publications 1995.
3 John Richardson *A history of Camden* Historical Publications 1999.
4 E Grey *St Giles's of the Lepers* Longmans 1905.
5 *Survey of London, Vol III Parish of St Giles-in-the-Fields* LCC 1912.
6 Camden History Society *Streets of St Giles* 2000.
7 C Gordon *Old time Aldwych, Kingsway and neighbourhood* Fisher, Unwin 1905
8 Ref.5, p 33 and ref.7 give the name as John Iffrey.
9 E Beresford Chancellor *The romance of Lincoln's Inn Fields* Richards 1932
10 W Blott *A chronicle of Blemundsbury* The Author 1892.
11 W Paxon *Brief history of the Baptist Chapel in Little Wild Street* G Wightman 1835.
12 C Woollacott *A brief history of the Baptist Church in Little Wild Street, Lincoln's Inn Fields 1691–1858* Christopher London 1858.
13 E Walford *Old London – Covent Garden and the Thames to Whitehall* Alderman Press reprint, 1987.
14 M Gaskell *Slums* Leicester University 1990.
15 H Morley 'Conversion of a heathen Court' in *Household Words* 1854 No.247 Vol. X pp 409–413
16 H Morley 'Wild Court tamed' in *Household Words* 1855 No.283 Vol. XII pp 85–87.
17 London Metropolitan Archives' *Plans of sites, session 1881-2 SBL 1566A* gives a breakdown of the owners, lessees and occupiers and contains a site plan.

18 LMA (SBL 1566 A); The school is mentioned in the Post Office Directory until 1935; from then on it is described as the LCC Handicraft Centre. Confusingly, The London School Board kept publishing the last set of pupil figures in their Annual reports until 1940.

Other sources

Records of the London School Board: Published minutes of Proceedings (open access, 22.05); Book of Reference session 1882 (SBL 1546); published Annual Reports.
British Biographical Index (microfiche).
City Literary Institute *City Lit Prospectuses* 1948–99.
E de Maré *The London Doré saw* Allen Lane 1973.
H Dyos *Exploring the urban past* Cambridge UP 1982.
A Lohrli *Household Words... a Weekly Journal 1850–59 conducted by Charles Dickens: Table of contents, list of contributors and their contributions* University of Toronto 1973.
T Williams *The City Literary Institute* 1960.

Geraldine Charles is an archivist at the National Maritime Museum. Since 1996 she has sung with *The City Lit 'A capella' group*, which is based at Keeley House.

Rise and fall of the Aerated Bread Company

by Robert Leon

In 1991 there were 59 McDonalds restaurants in London (counting postal districts only); today that total has risen to 106. London, together with the rest of Britain and indeed Europe, has gone 'burger-mad'. The ubiquitous manifestation of a familiar sign over a restaurant door, the promise of relatively fast service and the absence of the formal trappings of the more traditional restaurant have combined to endow the hamburger chain with phenomenal popularity. Phenomenal it may be, but as a previous generation of Londoners will confirm, not unprecedented: the ABC pioneered this form of mass catering over 100 years ago – with, by comparison, even more spectacular results.

The nature of the Company was complex, and there were frequent changes in its trading policy, so that the pattern of distribution of ABC bakeries and tearooms changed from one decade to another. In this article I draw attention to these changes and try to explain the demise of this highly successful Camden industry, setting the company within the broader context of the industry. But which industry?

The question must be put because, although the company name reflects the importance of the mass-production bakery, most people remember a restaurant or a convenient stop for a cup of tea. Nevertheless, the compilers of the London Directories listed the company under *Bakers*, and it is with the bread that one must begin. What *was* 'aerated bread', and why there was a market for it?

A new bread

The demand for aerated bread arose from an aversion among some people towards yeast. The prevailing form of leaven in the early 19th century was brewer's yeast, which provoked something of a crisis of conscience for those who were the most scrupulous of abstainers. At the same time there was a growing realisation that many of the strictures placed on the consumption of certain foods for religious purposes had their origins in wise precautions adopted amongst primitive societies for sound hygienic reasons. These prejudices were confirmed by the publication of theories of, amongst others, Pasteur (1857) and Eben Horsford at Harvard University (1861), who both affirmed that fermentation by yeast involved microscopic organisms comparable with mould or fungi. The problem was how, without the use of yeast, one could create the gases necessary to make the bread rise.

The solution came with the employment of fizzy water. Joseph Priestley had discovered a method of artificially carbonating water in 1767 and this was now used to replace ordinary water in a bread mix with the intention of producing a gaseous dough. The rest is Camden History. The method was first developed by Luke Hebert of Paternoster Row, who patented it in 1836 but was unable to apply it successfully in a bakery, the problem being that the fizzy water tended to go flat. It was John Dauglish, an eccentric but nevertheless brilliant doctor and inventor, who perfected the method: he mixed the water and other ingredients in a pressurised container so that, when the dough was finally released, the gas was able to expand, providing the necessary lift.[1] The Dauglish family established the Aerated Bread Company, but not everyone thanked them for it: many considered the new bread tasteless. One may wonder whether, if the success of the company had rested solely on the popularity of the bread, profits would have justified the investment which culminated 60 year later in the enormous building which became a Camden landmark (Fig 1).

The bakery shops

In fact, the Company's first bakeries were opened not in Camden but on the fringe of the City, in the area now buried under the Barbican. The 1864 London Directory lists 15 branches, of which two were in City Road and Upper Street, Islington. Only one branch was in Central London, at 79 Tottenham Court Road; another, in what is modern Camden, was in Euston Road. At this time the total number of bakery outlets listed in London was 2542, so ABC represented a mere 0.6% of the total.

By 1871 the number of ABC branches had increased to 88, including several more immediately to the north of the City: Fore Street; Gloucester Street, Clerkenwell; Goswell Road; Gray's Inn Road; Leather Lane; Myddleton Street and Old Street Road. By now the first bakery had been opened in Camden, in Park Street (subsequently Park Way), and this served the ABC shops in the north-west: Euston Road; Henry Street, St John's Wood; Highgate Road and Malden Road in Kentish Town.

As Londoners moved out to the suburbs, the number of bakeries in the central area fell slightly to 2521, and the ABC's 88 branches now represented 3.5% of the total. The decline

1   The ABC bakery in Camden Town, 1924–1982. It replaced the various buildings which the Company had previously assembled on this site.

Table 1 London baking and catering outlets 1864–1891
(bakers, refreshment rooms, coffee rooms and dining rooms listed in London directories)

	1864	1871	1881	1891
Bakeries	2542	2521	2350	2068
Refreshment Rooms	44	132	292	377
Coffee Rooms	1507	1571	1727	1744
Dining Rooms	367	401	457	678

in the number of London's bakery outlets continued into the next decade, by which time the company had added 19 more branches and the ABC share was now 4.5%. In modern Camden, the number of ABC outlets had risen to 8: Euston Road, Goodge Street, Gray's Inn Road, Hampstead Road, Malden Road, Marchmont Street, Theobald's Road and Tottenham Court Road.

By 1891 the Company's production capacity had been concentrated on to the new site on Camden Road, which would gradually be extended. This represented an important change of policy so that, instead of eight bakeries spread around London serving local groups of shops, ABC now had a single factory capable of supplying the whole chain. The total number of London bakery outlets had fallen further to 2068, with ABC still accounting for 3.5%. Now there was a drastic change of location policy which complemented the concentration of production in Camden. The Company divested itself of many of its distant branches, directing its resources towards maximising its presence in Central London. The number of ABC branches was reduced to 96, but there were many more in the City: 49 as against 1881's 14. At the same time many of the branches in East London and south of the Thames were jettisoned, and the ABC name disappeared from areas such as Bermondsey, Battersea, Poplar, Stepney, Wandsworth, Walworth and Lambeth.

Catering in London

Camden residents may associate ABC with the large bakery which dominated Camden Road, but for many Londoners the firm signified a chain of restaurants offering meals at affordable prices. There was no category *restaurants* in the trades listed in the London Directories for 1864 or 1871; instead, reference is made to the categories *Refreshment Rooms, Dining Rooms* and *Coffee Rooms*.

Restaurants in hotels, and gentlemen's clubs, offered a sophisticated brand of catering, with a considerable gap between the standard of these establishments and the average low chophouse; and London offered very few places where men and women could dine together in public. However, Dining Rooms were an increasingly prominent feature of London life: Table 1 shows the contrast between the decline in the number of bakeries and the rise in eating places. Of the streets where the ABC had their first outlets, the City Road, perhaps because of its length, was the best endowed with dining rooms, there being 1 in 1864, 2 in 1871, 6 in 1881 and 5 in 1891. When the Company opened branches in Aldersgate and Bishopsgate, the ABC was entering areas already replete with dining rooms: 8 and 7 respectively for these two streets.

Refreshment Rooms were also very much a feature of Central London and increasing in number (Table 1). Of the streets where ABC had outlets, the Strand contained the greatest number of refreshment rooms: 2 in 1871, 12 in 1881 and 17 in 1891, or 4.5% of the London total.

In contrast to dining and refreshment rooms, coffee rooms had already reached a substantial total before ABC was founded (Table 1), the greatest number in the long roads that ran through densely populated areas: in 1881 there were 21 in Commercial Road, 19 in Old Kent Road, 18 in Hackney Road and 12 in Euston Road. The same roads were well served by bakers in 1881: 15 in Commercial Road, 23 in the Old Kent Road and 18 in Hackney Road, but none in Euston Road. Significantly therefore, when the ABC changed policy and opted for

more branches in Central London, the Company was abandoning areas where bakers and coffee rooms abounded, concentrating instead on the places where dining rooms (and, later, restaurants) were flourishing, together with refreshment rooms. One notable exception was Roman Road, where the branch was retained; here there were 15 bakers and 7 coffee rooms in 1891.

Evidently, coffee rooms were concentrated close to where people lived whereas dining and refreshment rooms were opened with a view to serving the traveller, business man or the occasional visitor to the West End.

New locations

The new ABC policy was continued up to World War I, with further premises for dining rooms acquired in Central London such as Pall Mall and Regent Street; in 1914 the Company had 134 branches. After the War a certain amount of retrenchment was inevitable and in 1921 the number of branches fell back to 108, a figure which included 15 new branches; some of these were in areas abandoned at the time of the first bout of rationalisation 20 years before. ABC was back in Holloway Road, and also further out in Seven Sisters Road; the Company had returned to Kentish Town and reached Kilburn High Road. Of the outlets that had disappeared, 12 were in the City. Meanwhile, existing branches were regenerated and upgraded throughout the 1920s; the most conspicuous example was at the Wilton Road branch, near Victoria Station, which became the flagship of the Company under the name 'Empire Restaurant'.

During the 1930s ABC expanded beyond the boundaries of 19th-century London, following the pattern of suburban development and often going beyond it, so that the ABC came to be considered a regional company rather than one confined to the capital. Within London a few inner suburbs still not represented in the ABC portfolio – Balham, Brixton, Chiswick, Hammersmith, Lewisham, Peckham, Putney and Tooting – were added before World War II.

After the war there was a gradual withdrawal from prestigious addresses in Central London (Cheapside, Gresham Street, Brompton Road) that the Company had occupied since before World War I. In 1971, out of 162 London branches, only 17 were in the area bounded by Euston Road, Whitechapel, Gloucester Road and the Thames. New branches were often acquired by taking over existing bakeries, and there was steady expansion in the northern outer suburbs (Table 2).

Table 2 London locations of Lyons and ABC branches

	ABC Central	ABC Other	Lyons Central	Lyons Other
1864	7	8	-	-
1871	32	56	-	-
1881	38	69	-	-
1891	65	15	-	-
1901	89	20	31	4
1911	106	28	123	29
1921	92	24	113	40
1931	85	36	115	78
1941	93★	44★	99	79
1951	47★	35★	93	83

★ These figures refer to London Directory listings only and do not include branches in Middlesex and Essex.

The competition

It is at this point that a useful comparison may be made with the firm of J.Lyons, which opened its first branch in 1894, in Piccadilly. From the outset Lyons concentrated its efforts in Central London, where they were competing with ABC for prime sites: within 12 years they had opened their first 100 branches and all but 21 were in the City, Westminster or the West End (Table 2). Of the inner suburbs, Kensington was the most favoured location, three of their branches being in Brompton Road and one in the High Street. Of the 79 Lyons branches in Central London, 26 were in streets where the ABC was not represented, 15 of them being in the City. In Queen Victoria Street two Lyons branches were opened, in 1894 and 1901. Competition was keenest in the Strand, where ABC had 8 outlets and Lyons 4. In Oxford Street Lyons had the edge with 5 branches as against ABC's 3. This may suggest that Lyons aimed to attract shoppers rather than travellers through Charing

Cross. ABC was also dominant in Cannon Street, where there were 5 branches compared with only one Lyons.

In North London ABC still held the more prominent position. Lyons had branches in Edgware Road and Upper Street, Islington but otherwise nothing beyond the line of Marylebone, Euston and City Roads. Apart from Camden Road, ABC were represented in Dalston Lane, Drummond Street, Edgware Road, Hampstead Road, Pentonville Road and Upper Street.

After World War I, the ABC began to retreat from the City but Lyons did not: of their first 100 branches, 47 were in the City and 21 lasted to World War II, some beyond. Branches closed were often soon replaced: thus although two early branches in King William Street were closed by 1920 two others had been opened there.

The Camden bakery

The first ABC Bakery in Camden had served as a small manufacturing unit for a number of shops in North West London and in this respect was similar to others in Whitecross Street, Little Pulteney Street, Westminster Bridge Road, Cambridge Road and Beech Street. Several of these supplied many more shops than the Camden factory and must be presumed to have been bigger. The choice of Camden as the site for the new bakery to serve the whole ABC group was not automatic, therefore; proximity to the canal may have been a significant consideration. Since the timing of the choice coincided with the change of policy towards locating branches in Central London, it may be assumed that ease of access to it was an important factor – although the Glasgow firm of Stevenson, most of whose branches were also in Central London, chose Battersea for the site of their mammoth bakery.

The new ABC factory was built during a period of dramatic change for bakers, brought about by extensive mechanisation of the industry. Mixing, kneading, rolling and moulding of the dough was now done by machines, while the increasing sophistication of gas ovens meant that steam could be judiciously introduced during the baking process to improve the quality of the final product. This 'new age' of technology was propitious for capital investment in large bread factories, and several appeared on the London scene – but the amount of bread consumed annually by the average person had begun to fall.

Logistics of delivery

During the decades following World War I, the nature of ABC's business was transformed. Its branches were now spread over a very wide area, and it had to supply premises that were in many cases restaurants as well as bakery shops. This posed acute delivery problems, not least because the Company's fleet of vehicles was unsuitable for the range and type of its products.

At Camden Road the Company had huge freezers for storing fresh meat and fish, which were packed in metal containers for delivery to branches; however, the delivery vans were not refrigerated, so almost all the loading of vehicles had to take place in the early morning of the day of delivery.

Each vehicle, together with the driver and often a van boy or delivery assistant, was allocated to a particular route, supplying the same shops and restaurants daily. Semi-perishable foods such as potatoes and other vegetables were loaded the previous night but meat, fish and baked goods were loaded very early in the morning so that the van could leave the Camden Road yard by 6.30 am. All the metal trays containing fish and meat were loaded on one side of the van while the bread and cakes were put on the other.

Because the vans left Camden Road so early, they often arrived at the branches before they were open; to facilitate delivery, each driver had a spare key to the branch enabling him to enter. The van's delivery route would be completed in the morning and the van would be back in Camden by noon. The driver had probably been on duty since 5 am, and his day would now be finished unless he had volunteered for overtime, undertaking the afternoon deliveries of non-perishable items (tinned and dried goods), not necessarily to the same branches each day, for few branches needed a daily delivery of non-perishable goods.[2]

This complex delivery system, necessitating differing arrangements for four types of food product, cried out for some form of rationalisation. The restaurants needed an early delivery of meat and fish in order to prepare lunch. If the meat and fish were not delivered with the bakery goods but were obtained from an outside supplier, the ABC restaurant would have had to place a minimum order, and then would have needed a frozen-food store, a considerable investment at that time. An alternative course of action would have been to purchase a separate fleet of vehicles to deliver meat and fish only, but these would have had to be refrigerated, which would also have been costly. On the other hand, to have the delivery fleet back in the Camden yard by midday and some of them idle for the rest of the day meant that ABC were not deriving the maximum benefit from their vehicles.

The ABC is sold

After World War II, the baking industry was in depression because of the continuation of bread rationing. When normal trading resumed, it became apparent that some drastic changes would have to be made, and in 1955 ABC was acquired by Allied Bakeries, a branch of a Canadian company which also had substantial milling interests. Before World War II this company had already purchased 17 bakeries in Britain which all used home-produced flour. Garfield Weston, the head of what had become a multiple bread-producing company, now demanded discounts on his purchases from the principal millers such as Ranks and Spillers. The millers refused and, seeing that Weston could supply his bakeries from Canada if necessary, began themselves to acquire large bread factories to protect their share of the national flour market. However, while most of the nation's major bread suppliers passed into the hands of the principal milling groups, the amount of bread consumed nationally continued to fall (the national consumption of wheat flour, which had increased during the privations of war, would shortly fall below the 1934 level), so that the 1950s witnessed a frantic rush on the part of the millers to acquire large bakery firms solely for the amount of flour that they consumed. The ABC became one of the most famous victims of this take-over mania.

From the point of view of the new proprietors, the value of ABC now lay in the amount of flour consumed in the Camden bakery. However, Allied Bakeries also had other substantial factories in the London area, notably Broomfields in Greenwich and Coombs in Twickenham. The opportunities for economies of scale, combined with the continuing fall in bread consumption, ensured that a period of rationalisation would follow.

By 1976 the Camden workforce had dramatically declined. The ABC name itself would shortly disappear, for by now Allied Bakeries needed a new generation of bakeries with easy access to motorways, such as their new factory in Stevenage. The ABC Camden bakery closed in 1982. In the light of the subsequent redevelopment of the site, the success enjoyed by the new Sainsbury building, and the gradual regeneration of Camden Town itself, it is difficult now to imagine how the factory survived so long in such a valuable location. The writing had been on the bakery wall long before the various post-war explosions in property values. Recalling with nostalgia that the ABC was a well-known institution only 18 years ago obscures the fact that the building in Camden was already an anachronism in terms of the effective production and delivery of baked goods.

ABC and Lyons compared

Table 3 shows that in 1971 the

Table 3 Location of Lyons and ABC branches in 1971

	Lyons	ABC
City of London	12	4
Rest of Central London	19	11
Kensington and Chelsea	5	3
Inner northern suburbs	2	24
Outer northern suburbs	3	59
Inner eastern suburbs	1	4
Outer eastern suburbs	4	12
Inner southern suburbs	4	6
Outer southern suburbs	11	4
Inner western suburbs	3	11
Outer western suburbs	0	15
Totals	64	153

2   The ABC teashop in Bishopsgate, 1925. The writing over the door states that the Head Office is in Camden Road. On the window the Company advertises a Ladies' Room and a Smoking Room inside.

3   Same premises as in Fig 2 in 1959, showing the new ABC logo. This branch became a *Baker's Oven* and is now one of the *Prêt à Manger* branches.

individual paths followed by these companies had led to a very different distribution of their outlets. Lyons had held on to many of their Central London locations whereas ABC now had substantial representation in the outer suburbs, particularly in North London. Neither company had many branches in South London although Lyons had had a teashop in Croydon since 1901.

Like the ABC, Lyons also had a very large bread-baking operation which, in addition to supplying the restaurants and tea shops, delivered to homes; later this was expanded, so that the firm became substantial bread wholesalers. ABC, on the other hand, for the most part concentrated on supplying their own outlets.

Both companies slowly converted their outlets to self-service, the precursor of the modern fast-food restaurant. Lyons closed their last teashop in 1981, but a number of the ABC premises (e.g. Fig 2) were revamped by Allied Bakeries (Fig 3) and given a new lease of life as the Baker's Oven chain, which survived when Allied Bakeries disposed of the business to Greggs, a company based in Newcastle. Lyons also became a major food-processing company; this may have distracted the company from paying proper attention to its restaurant business. It may be also that ABC's obligation to keep the Camden bakery turning over ultimately prevented ABC from developing into a dynamic modern catering firm. It is interesting to reflect that while the creation of the Lyons baking factory stemmed from its need to supply a chain of restaurants and tea shops, the ABC restaurant chain grew out of the scale and success of the Camden bakery. In their heyday, London supported the two greatest catering institutions of any city in the world but, ultimately, the failure to concentrate effectively on the provision of a modern catering service in tune with popular demand led to the disappearance of both.

London certainly lost something with the demise of these reasonably priced restaurants. Food for thought as we tuck into our next Big Mac!

Notes

1   Neither Hebert nor Dauglish was concerned about the possible dangers of consuming yeast-based products. Both considered that the principal benefit of their methods was a reduction in production costs, although Dauglish also wished to minimise contact of the dough with the skin of bakery workers. Working conditions in commercial bakeries were notoriously unhygienic.

2   I am grateful to Mr George Green of Hampstead for his generous help in providing information concerning the working and delivery arrangements at ABC.

Sources

Post Office directories, especially for 1864, 1871, 1881, 1891
Peter Bird *The first food empire* Phillimore 2000 (complete history of J.Lyons)
Elizabeth David *English bread and yeast cookery* Penguin 1979 (explanation of the importance of Dauglish and aerated bread)
Eveley & Little *Concentration in British industry* Cambridge UP 1960 (rationalisation of modern food-processing factories and their location near motorways)
Robert Leon *Since sliced bread* Unpublished thesis, University of London
William Peter Maunder *The bread industry in the United Kingdom* University of Nottingham 1970 (the battle fought by the major milling groups to acquire the large bakeries)

Robert Leon worked in the baking industry for 15 years. In 2000 he co-ordinated the Camden History Society's Millennium Project. He has lived in West Hampstead for 16 years.

Camden History Society Occasional paper 3

Victorian Seven Dials
a portrait based on contemporary accounts

David A Hayes

Just published by The Camden History Society

see overleaf for further details

order your copy now

Victorian Seven Dials

In this, the third of Camden History Society's series of Occasional Papers, David Hayes has transcribed and annotated the manuscript of an address of 1865 in which a young evangelist appealed for funds, vividly evoking the district around Seven Dials and its colourful, indigent inhabitants. Hayes's scholarly footnotes amplify this portrait with quotations from Dickens, Charles Booth, Henry Mayhew and other 19th-century authors. The text is amply illustrated with historical and current prints and photographs.

The original Seven Dials monument at the centre of the area was erected in 1694. It was surmounted by sundials, hence the name, but there were only six of them – since only six streets were originally planned to converge on the circular space it occupied.

The monument itself had long disappeared by 1865, but it was re-created from plans held by the British Museum and unveiled in 1989. Functional as well as decorative, 17th-century sundial pillars were constructed in order to regulate London's public clocks, which were becoming increasingly popular but were inaccurate and unreliable. The re-created sundials at Seven Dials were ingeniously calibrated so that *between them* (and weather permitting), they accurately record the time throughout daylight hours. In the middle of a sunny summer day the southerly dials are so placed that they correctly show the (Greenwich Mean) time; the more northerly ones come into play only in the morning and evening.

Historical details of the area surrounding Seven Dials district, namely the rest of the parish of St Giles-in-the-Fields, may be found in *Streets of St Giles* (Camden History Society, 2000).

£5.95
plus postage